THE ACTS OF THE APOSTLES

NEW TESTAMENT FOR SPIRITUAL READING

VOLUME 10

Edited by

John L. McKenzie, S.J.

THE ACTS
OF THE APOSTLES

Volume I

JOSEF KÜRZINGER

CROSSROAD · NEW YORK

2578

1981
The Crossroad Publishing Company
575 Lexington Avenue, New York, NY 10022

Originally published as *Die Apostelgeschichte 1*
© 1966 by Patmos-Verlag
from the series *Geistliche Schriftlesung*
edited by Wolfgang Trilling
with Karl Hermann Schelke and Heinz Schürmann

English translation © 1969 by Burns & Oates, Limited, London
Translated by Anthony N. Fuerst

Library of Congress Catalog Card Number: 81-68167
ISBN: 0-8245-0119-5

PREFACE

The book of Acts is the second of a two-volume work written by Luke, identified elsewhere in the New Testament (Colossians 4:14; 2 Timothy 4:11; Philemon 24) as a companion of Paul. Luke is the only one of the evangelists who conceived of the life of Jesus and the beginnings of the church as a single series of events. The two works are joined by a reference in Luke 24:47 to the proclamation of repentance and forgiveness in the name of Jesus to all nations, beginning from Jerusalem, and a reference in Acts 1:8 to the witness of the apostles in Jerusalem, Judea, Samaria and to the end of the earth. In both of these verses the geographical references follow the structure of the book of Acts. Since the book was written some years after the events with which the book concludes, it is an ancient puzzle why Luke chose to end the narrative where he did, with no reference to the further expansion of the church and to the martyrdom of Paul, who is the central personage of most of the narrative. It is most probable that Luke considered that Rome, the center of Mediterranean government and civilization, fulfilled the definition of " the ends of the earth," since from Rome as a center the church could grow to all parts of the Roman Empire.

The Gospel is the book of the Lord; Acts is the book of the Spirit. Luke alone has the narrative of Pentecost; without this power from on high (Luke 24:49; Acts 1:8) the apostles were unable to proclaim and bear witness. No other New Testament writer except Paul, Luke's master in the gospel and in the missions, has so many references to the Spirit as the principle of Christian life and the Christian mission. The theme of the Spirit as the power in the church which continues the life and work of

v

Jesus is also found in the gospel of John (14–16). Even Gamaliel recognized that the mission was the work of God, not of men (Acts 5:38–39).

Paul is the central figure of the narrative after chapter 12 because it was Paul who was most active in carrying the gospel from Jerusalem, Judea and Samaria to the end of the earth. He was the chosen apostle of the gentiles (Galatians 2:8). He certainly was not the only apostle of the gentiles; the names of the founders of most of the early Christian communities are unknown, and most of them were founded by some one other than Paul. It was not the intention of Luke to write a complete history of the first Christian missions, and no other writer attempted the task. Historically we are poorer for this omission; but in the book of Acts, as in the gospels, we are dealing with works which are not primarily historical. Paul was the most representative of the apostles; Luke says nothing of any mission of any of the Twelve outside of Judea and Samaria. And with reference to the mission of Judea and Samaria, he mentions only Peter and John by name.

Luke obviously presents the church of Jerusalem as the model Christian community; and there is some question about the extent to which he has idealized this community, which must have been totally destroyed when the book was written. There is also some question how much personal acquaintance Luke had with this community. The communal poverty which Luke describes in Jerusalem is not only not attested of any other Christian community, but is not mentioned of Jerusalem in any other New Testament book. With this goes the peculiar emphasis on poverty and the poor in the gospel of Luke. Similarly Luke attributes to Jerusalem an inner unity and harmony which leaves no room for dissension. This too has its connections. Explicit in several of the epistles of Paul and implicit in some other books is the division between Jewish and gentile Christians in the first generation of the apostolic church. In Acts this division is neatly and cleanly settled by a deliberation in the Jerusalem church. Everything indicates that the settlement of the problem was much more complex than it appears to be in the narrative of Luke. Indeed, that the settlement so easily reached in chapter 15 was not definitive is implied in the account of Paul's visit to Jerusalem in 21 : 20-24.

The power of the Spirit resides in the gospel, which is itself a word of power. It does not compel belief, but it compels to a decision. When it is proclaimed, innocent and ignorant unbelief are no longer possible. The power is not dependent on the power and skill of the speaker, a theme which Paul also emphasized (1 Corinthians 2 : 1-6). Wherever Paul proclaimed the gospel, a permanent church was founded. The word of the gospel is in a sense identified with Jesus himself; to believe in the gospel and to believe in Jesus are used interchangeably. The gospel is not the story of Jesus nor the memory of Jesus; it is the confrontation with the personal reality of Jesus, and the eyewitnesses believe no more and no less than those to whom they proclaim their witness. The believers encounter Jesus in the proclamation and in the church.

Luke is the only New Testament writer who calls Christianity " The Way." It certainly appears more as a way of life than as a rigorously structured society. It is difficult to identify officers and functions in the church of Acts; and it is no easier in the other New Testament books. Once Paul had founded a community, he exercised no government over it. Each local church elected its own officers, whose titles and functions are quite vague, and it was left as an independent self-sufficient entity. " Self-sufficiency " is not meant to deny that the life of the local church depended on its communion with other churches; and the idea of " the church " as one great whole appears in the New Testament. But the churches were self-sufficient in the sense that they depended on no other church for their belief and their worship. Each local church offered to its members the fullness of the Christian life; no church, not even the church of Jerusalem, was more " Christian " than any other church. The absence of numerous and clear references to figures of authority leave the impression that the churches of Acts were quite democratic in character, particularly in contrast to the contemporary Roman Catholic Church. The apostolic church sensed no need for centralized authority either in the church as a whole or in the local churches.

Luke can be an extremely realistic narrator. He follows the practice of Greek and Roman historians of composing speeches for his characters. Recent studies indicate that these speeches are not purely the product of Luke's imagination, but are the best examples of the apostolic proclamation or preaching, the *kerygma*. This does not apply, of course, to the several speeches attributed to Paul in the course of his hearings before Jewish and Roman authorities. Luke also composes dialogue readily and with realism; and many of his scenes have a rare dramatic quality. The persons themselves emerge as real persons. The Paul of Acts appears as the same man who wrote the epistles, even though Luke in relation to the epistles raises several problems concerning details in the life of Paul. Here also Luke allows himself the same freedom in the handling of events which we have noticed for other themes of the book of Acts.

Acts is in the last analysis a narrative of its own type, difficult to classify with other narratives. The freedom of treatment compels us to regard the book as an imaginative rather than a realistic and factual account. One must attend to the theological intentions and themes of Luke unless one wishes to misunderstand him.

JOHN L. McKENZIE, S.J.

INTRODUCTION

The Acts of the Apostles is a book of the New Testament for which readers show a decided preference. The uninitiated in the art of reading the Bible especially will receive through its pages a knowledge of and an orientation to the whole of the New Testament. Its manner of presentation is easy to grasp; its literary arrangement is readily perceptible. Through it we obtain insight into the salvific work of God in Jesus Christ and into the salvific economy of the church which is built upon him.

What does the Acts of the Apostles intend to convey? The title may deceive us. For it is not concerned—as its title might lead us to expect—with the personal fate or with the work of the individual apostles. Only two of them play parts worthy of note, namely, Peter and John, but even of these John appears principally as a companion to Peter. On the other hand, other personages pass before our eyes: the first seven official collaborators of the apostles (6—8) and after them Barnabas and Saul. By far the largest part of the book is devoted to the latter, upon whom the title of apostle was bestowed by reason of his special call by Christ himself.

What should we understand by the title? In ancient Grecian manuscripts the book bears the title *Praxis*, and in this form it corresponds to similar headings in apocryphal Greek literature. It may be that this title was given to the work by the author himself, since he was familiar with hellenic culture. It deals, consequently, with " actions," with " happenings," and with

" events." The Acts was also called " Deeds "—in Latin, *Acta*.
These " deeds " have one thing in common : they center on and
are connected with the apostles; they treat of a " history " in
which they took an active part.

Jerusalem and Rome are the twin poles between which this
history unrolls geographically. The first thirty years after the
ascension of our Lord form its chronological framework. This
history is not an unbroken narrative after the fashion of a
chronicle; it is not narration of all that actually happened.
Isolated portraits are sketched, rather important moments serve
to disclose the mystery of the church in ever new dimensions.

The mystery of the church as the Acts of the Apostles sees it
is Christ the Lord. He stands at its beginning not only because
of the commission which he bestowed and the promise which he
made, but also because he manifests his presence in the " Holy
Spirit." The tidings of the *Pneuma hagion,* the living breath
and the creative spirit of God, but at the same time " the spirit
of Christ " (Rom. 8 : 9), are the special concern of the Acts of the
Apostles. With good reason, then, these Acts are called the
" gospel of the Holy Spirit." This " Spirit " is that power which
from the very beginning filled the church and protected her
from what was merely human; the Spirit who especially in
moments of danger outwardly manifested his presence. The
principal objective of this book is to show that in spite of
opposition and of persecution from without and in spite of all
crises and threats from within—in fact, precisely because of them
—the Church grew and gained in strength. The grandiose task
of the apostles to witness to the world (1 : 8) is consequently
intimately bound up with the promise " of the power of the Holy
Spirit who will be poured out over them."

It is true, of course, that the author shows a truly self-sacrificing interest in the development and expansion of the mother community in Jerusalem and describes the development of the church in Palestino-Syrian territory. But quickly thereafter he turns his attention, his entire attention, to one man, Saul, through whom the church was guided away from its Judeo-Christian beginnings and threatening insularity and brought to unfold a world-spanning mission.

This should not surprise us. For the author is Luke, the physician whose intimate partnership with Paul is attested to by the letters of the Apostle as he languished in prison (Col. 4:14; Phm. 24; 2 Tim. 4:11). This fellowship began when around A.D. 44, together with Barnabas, Paul labored in Antioch, which tradition teaches us was the home of Luke and where the first gentile Christian community was founded (11:25). With this in mind we can readily understand the special interest of the Acts of the Apostles in the travels and labors of the Apostle of the gentiles. From chapter 13 onward and even more from chapter 22 to the end, the narrative reads as if it were the speech of a lawyer who was trying to prove how great were the missionary accomplishments of his client and his personal and legal-political inassailability as he whiled away his time in prison.

When did Luke write this work? The answer is not without importance for correct understanding of the book itself. What has the Acts itself to tell us on this matter? Seven chapters (22–28) occupy themselves exclusively with narrating the various places in which the Apostle was detained—places where he was juridically examined for the purpose of establishing his guilt or innocence, a process which lasted almost five years. The last two years in Rome are passed over rather lightly, few words being devoted to their history. We learn scarcely anything about what happened in those years. There are no accounts and no indications which deal with the judicial process (and charges brought against Paul) which up to this point had been depicted so graphically. Neither is the outcome of the case given us. Perhaps the book was written while the sentence was being awaited from the imperial court to which Paul had appealed. Or perhaps Luke realized that in that highly placed man to whom he had dedicated his gospel (Lk. 1 : 3) and whom he again mentions by name at the beginning of the Acts of the Apostles, namely, Theophilus (who was friendly and well-disposed to the Christian cause), he had on his side a person who was in a position to exercise considerable influence in hastening the process along and in bringing it to a successful conclusion. On such a supposition, it would have been towards the end of the year A.D. 63 that the Acts of the Apostles was written—an opinion which had previously been generally accepted.

We would subscribe to this view were it not for objections which render such an early date untenable. The gospel of Luke, which was anterior to the Acts of the Apostles, could not have been composed before the destruction of Jerusalem, in the year A.D. 70. External witnesses of tradition and intrinsic character-istics of the gospel itself bear this out. Once this reasoning is accepted, it would follow that the Acts of the Apostles could not have been written before, only after A.D. 70. According to most scholars, therefore, the Acts originated about the year A.D. 80.

OUTLINE

THE MOTHER COMMUNITY IN JERUSALEM
(1:1—5:42)

Awaiting the Holy Spirit (1:1-26)

Promise and Mission (1:1-11)

The first eleven verses of the Acts of the Apostles refer almost
directly to what was said previously in Luke 24. This was done
not simply for repetition's sake, but to furnish us with a résumé
and connective in which we can apprehend the deep concerns
of the author more clearly.

These concerns center upon the coming of the Holy Spirit.
Luke attempts to show that the resurrection is not only a glorious
and fitting climax to the life of Christ, but also, and at the same
time, that it is the life-producing and salvific reason for the
existence of the church. The " new creation " (Rom. 6:4; Gal.
6:5) here receives its reality and its true finality. We should not
be disturbed to discover that not every detail provided in the
introduction agrees precisely with the details of the same event
in Luke 24; for we must remember that the introduction looks
backward. In handing on the " glad tidings " in which he dis-
plays a praiseworthy trustworthiness, Luke worked as a descrip-
tive and talented narrator, free of bias and extremely candid.

THE GOSPEL IN RETROSPECT (1:1-3)

¹In my first book, Theophilus, I gave an account of all that Jesus did and taught, ²up to the day on which he was taken up into heaven, after he had through the Holy Spirit given a mission to the apostles.

We know of this first report, or " first book," through the gospel according to St. Luke, which is known to all the world. We should read this gospel attentively if we are to gain a truly deep insight into the Acts of the Apostles. For both these books are in harmony one with the other not only by reason of literary style—and this despite all the peculiarities of the gospel, conditioned as it is by the source from which it is drawn—but also because of their common religious concern.

The content of the gospel is summarized in the statement, " all that Jesus did and taught." This is an important and meaningful synthesis, one significant for early tradition. From the very beginning " deed " and " word " belonged to the mission, to the story of Jesus, and thereby also to the statements of the gospel; for by intrinsic necessity the " deeds " belong to the " words." And if the words of Jesus are harbingers of truth and salvation, they must also state clearly what he was and what he wished to reveal by his action. This is graphically attested to in the gospel of St. Mark, which is generally regarded as the oldest of the gospels. When we further consider that in the beginning the faithful gave their attention especially to the story of the passion, we can understand the interest which the first disciples paid to whatever happened to Jesus. Thus in the passage which we are now considering, there is a precedence of " what Jesus did " over " what he taught."

Also, the concisely worded intimation of some kind of framework (" from the beginning onward to the day on which he was taken up to heaven ") demonstrates how much Luke the evangelist is obligated to the restrictions and limitations which were observed in the *universal primitive proclamation* of the " good news." We meet this framework again in 1:21; and in the basic outline of the four gospels it is also clearly in the fore, with the narratives beginning with John the Baptist and concluding with the story of the Risen Lord. If in a backward glance at the " first narrative " we find nothing said of the infancy narrative of Jesus which is so intimately bound up with the gospel of Luke, this does not justify the conclusion that such a narrative was meaningless in the mind of the evangelist. It means only that it did not fit in with the basic plan of the message of the salvific activity of the Lord as sketched by the primitive church.

The day on which Jesus was " taken up into heaven " receives special and significant emphasis in the Acts of the Apostles by reason of the *mission entrusted to the apostles*. For the first time the men after whom the book is entitled are named. They did not take up their office out of personal choice; Jesus himself had " chosen them." This fact seems important to the evangelist. In his gospel we learn of the choice of the twelve " whom he also called apostles " (Lk. 6:12–16). It is also important to realize that apostleship dates back to the days of the pre-paschal Lord. Apostolic activity is entirely and personally linked to the earthly as well as with the transfigured Jesus, to his word, to his omnipotent power, to his full authority, and to his mission.

What is meant by the word " mission " (or commission)? The word is broad in connotation and possesses a variety of meanings which can be attached to all that Jesus bestowed as testament upon his disciples after his resurrection. If we should bear in mind the connection which exists between the sentence we are now considering and the subsequent one, we would not be far afield in concluding that the author thinks and speaks of a special mission, an entirely specific one. Moreover, the concluding words of the Risen One in the gospel inform us of this very mission, when it is reported, " And behold, I send you the promise of my Father. Remain in the city, until you are invested with power from on high " (Lk. 24:49). This " power from on high " is the Holy Spirit. The mission of Jesus to the apostles was directed towards this Spirit-power even before Jesus was taken up into heaven. We are justified, then, in thinking of this mission in terms of the Holy Spirit; and in fact the Greek grammar appears to recommend the following translation as the better: " through the (or: in the) Holy Spirit." By this translation it would be alleged that Jesus entrusted the disciples with this mission because he himself was filled with the Holy Pneuma (Spirit)—and this would put Lucan Christology in better light and grant it a fuller meaning. Another interpretation, however, nonetheless appears (despite grammatical considerations) to be more natural by reason of the entire text and in retrospect of the gospel: that the Holy Spirit is the content and the motive for this mission given on the day of his ascension into heaven. The following sentence makes this meaning still more evident.

³He also proved himself alive to them after his passion by showing them many proofs, appearing to them throughout forty days, and speaking to them of matters relating to the kingdom of God.

This verse also refers us back to what was said in the gospel. The trial of Jesus, his cross and his tomb, summarized in the phrase " his passion," had taken place, had become realities, and had been given an enriched meaning in his paschal return to life. It is important for the evangelist to be able to put this down on paper. For the choice and the mission of the apostles receive their true validity only by reason of the summons and the conversations of the *One who was truly alive.* " Life " means far more than Jesus' previous life, regained at the resurrection from the dead. Here his life is filled with and transfigured by the Divine Reality, by which Jesus reveals himself to his own.

The evangelist is in a position to be able to speak of many *proofs.* In other words, there were many more appearances than those to which the gospel alludes (Lk. 24). We may, if we wish, add the narratives of the other gospels, John's included, concerning this matter. Yet we know that we cannot arrive at a true figure simply by working a problem of addition. This would not produce satisfactory results because of the unique literary styles of the various narratives. We must also take into account Paul's reports, because they coordinate a remarkable series of appearances of the Risen One (1 Cor. 15:3-7). And his own confrontation with the Risen Saviour—although it took place only " after forty days "—must also be reckoned with (1 Cor. 15:8f.; 9:1).

Throughout forty days Jesus appeared to his apostles. This assertion is made only in the Acts of the Apostles. Later on we will find mention (13:3) of a less exact space of time, namely, " of many days " (13:31). In the gospel according to Luke, the appearances of the Risen Lord are narrated in such a way that one might even conclude that everything—including the ascension into heaven—occurred on one and the same day (Lk. 24). According to John, the post-paschal encounters with Christ are spread over a period of time, lasting more than a week. A longer period of time is also presumed in 1 Corinthians 15:5-7. When in the passage we are discussing, Luke—in accordance with his usual manner of presentation—clarifies the information contained in Luke 24 by stipulating a fixed period of " forty days," we are in no sense to recognize in this only his preference for symbolism. It is true, of course, that the number forty is frequently used in the Bible as a means of characterizing an especially meaningful period of time, as for example the flood (Gen. 8:6), or Moses' encounter with God (Ex. 24:18) and his fasting (Ex. 34:28), or Elijah wandering in the desert to the mountain of God (3 Kgs. 19:8), or the forty days' sojourn of Jesus in the desert (Lk. 4:2; Mt. 4:2). In this context, however, the thought of Pentecost which took place on the fiftieth day after Easter might have been codeterminative for the computation of " forty days." For linked to the feast of Pentecost is that important event, the sending of the Spirit, which looms so largely in the story of the apostles. Of this sending (mission) of the Spirit it is said that it would take place " not many days hence " (1:5). Moreover, the number forty may have suggested itself as a number, venerable by reason of tradition, to characterize the post-paschal days as being fruitful and decisive for the revelation and understanding of the mystery of Christ.

THE MISSION OF THE RISEN ONE (1:4–8)

[4]*And while he was staying with them, he instructed them, " Do not depart from Jerusalem, but await the promise of the Father, of which you have heard from me. [5]For John indeed baptized with water, but you shall be baptized with the Holy Spirit not many days hence."*

This scene was enacted on the day Christ " was taken up into heaven." The important instruction given in 1:2 is paraphrased here in more precise terms. In the gospel the same instruction is phrased somewhat differently, when it is stated, "Behold, I send you the promise of my Father; remain in the city until you are invested with power from on high" (Lk. 24:49). It is not at all disturbing when the same author, the same evangelist, repeats one and the same injunction in a different or free form. The primitive church did not take things too literally, for she was concerned more with the meaning than with the letter of tradition. This last *staying with them* was, according to another hypothesis or according to the original text, *a communal banquet* (*agape*). According to still another theory, the Risen Saviour had eaten in the presence of, and with, his disciples. Even during the time of his pre-paschal labors Jesus repeatedly linked important instructions and revelations to meals taken together with his apostles. In this connection we need but recall the Last Supper before the passion, when he released to them specific directions and handed over to them his last codicils. In its eucharistic festal meals the primitive church kept alive and dwelt upon the communal feasts at which the Risen Lord was present.

The order that the apostles were *to remain in Jerusalem* is peculiar to Luke. Though he knew well enough of a reference to Galilee (Lk. 24:6), in his narrative we can uncover no further hint of such a post-paschal encounter, although this is or was of importance to the other evangelists. We must view his delimiting of events to Jerusalem in light of his understanding of the salvific historic importance of Jerusalem, a fact that is clear in his gospel. In the prophecies of the Old Testament, which join together messianic salvation and the special gifts of salvation, we may find the reason for the preference for Jerusalem which Luke entertains. Luke knows that Jerusalem will be the starting point for the world-wide missionary labors of the church. As a consequence it is important for him to point out the way wending from Jerusalem to Rome.

The apostles should wait for the *promise of the Father*. The connection of events, the context, makes clear that the Holy Spirit is the one who is meant. He is the promise. All further phrases point expressly to him. He is the chief concern of the Risen Saviour. He is the " promise of the Father." The desig-nation of God simply as the Father, without a more precise qualifying term, is also used elsewhere, principally in the gospel of John. To what extent is the Holy Spirit " the promise of the Father "? We need but recall the words of the prophets in the Old Testament in which God foretold that the Holy Spirit would be the salvific gift of messianic times. In his farewell address Jesus spoke of the Spirit whom God would send. In this impe-tratory prayer he had said that " the Father will give the Holy Spirit to those who ask him " (Lk. 11:13). Before Easter the apostles had heard from the mouth of Jesus himself about the " promise of the Father."

Surprisingly, Jesus appropriates to himself the word of the Baptist concerning the coming of *a baptism of the Spirit* (Lk. 3:16). John the Baptist had alluded to the Messiah as one more powerful than himself: " I baptize you with water; but one stronger than I comes after me, the thong of whose sandal I am not worthy to untie; he will baptize you with the Holy Spirit and with fire " (Lk. 3:16). The message contained in the Baptist's words sought to point out the harmony existing between the reception of the Spirit which Jesus himself had experienced personally when he was baptized by John, and the baptism, impending for the apostles, which of necessity will have to be bestowed upon them if they are to fulfill the commission they are to be entrusted with.

⁶Those who now had come together, asked him, " Lord, will you at this time restore the kingdom of Israel?" ⁷He replied to them, " It is no concern of yours to know the times or the dates the Father has fixed by his authority which is peculiarly his own."

The query of the disciples is important, for in it there is embodied *a concept of the Messiah* which has its roots in both a politico-national and a religious obsession of a people oppressed for centuries. The dream of former greatness and of earlier autonomy as well as of a promising utopia in the messianic prophecies of the prophets gave free rein to hopes which must have been evoked by Jesus' presence. From Luke's own gospel we know of his constant warding off from Jesus all conjecture and all expectation of Jewish rationalization, so widespread among the people. As early in the public life of Jesus as the temptation in the desert, the concept of a religious Messiah is made evident (Lk. 4 : 5–8). And in fact, perhaps the importunate questioning of the apostles concerning the restoration of the kingdom of Israel has its justification in the words of the angel Gabriel at the time of the annunciation to Mary, when he said, " God the Lord will give him the throne of his father, David, and he will reign over the house of David forever, and of his kingdom there will be no end " (Lk. 1 : 32f.).

Was it not engrained in their way of thinking to pose such a question? For what else could the instruction to remain in Jerusalem and to await the baptism of the Spirit actually mean than that the fullness of time foretold by the prophets was about to be realized together with the gifts of salvation? Is not the

Risen One himself a sign that the new age had begun? In his answer Jesus pays less attention to the concept of Messiah than he does to the question concerning " this time."

Jesus' answer is meaningful and touches upon a burning concern of the early church—raises, in fact, the community's bruised spirits concerning the early arrival of the end of the world which the people of that era conceived as the " restoration of all things " (3:21). Are there not to be found in the gospel words of Jesus concerning the early advent of this glorious coming elements which nourished such a belief (Mk. 9:1; Lk. 21:32)? Does not Paul in his first letter show how even he was enthralled by the expectation of the Risen Christ coming again (1 Thess. 4:15)? So in the reply of Jesus—even though it does not supply us with direct information—we find some pertinent, important hints in answer to such queries about the end of time in its bearing on the history of salvation. " No one knows the day nor the hour, not even the angels in heaven, nor the Son, only the Father " (Mk. 13:32). In the face of the ever more clearly receding parousia of the Lord, the primitive church had to sate her yearning with the reverential knowledge that divine decrees are set apart by their exclusive competence and un-restricted freedom. Nevertheless, the church is charged with the task of waiting watchfully for the coming of the Lord.

[8]*" But you shall receive power, when the Holy Spirit descends upon you, and you shall be my witnesses in Jerusalem and in the whole of Judea and Samaria and even to the very ends of the earth."*

Here again it is of extreme importance to remember that the apostles will fulfill their task of witnessing by the *power* which they will receive, once the *Holy Spirit overshadows* them. This promise cannot be divorced from the task with which they are entrusted. This is the purpose of that " baptism of the Spirit " which they must receive " not many days hence." Not as mere men are they to give witness; he himself, the Lord, will accompany them. Though their personal experience is necessary, it is not of supreme importance. In 1:21 where the choice of the apostle, the new apostle, is narrated, this condition is expressly prescribed. But it is not without reason that the promise of the " power " of the Spirit precedes the passage concerning apostolic testimony. This idea of " awaiting " is several times amplified: " Do not depart from Jerusalem, but await the promise of the Father, of which you have heard from me " (1:4), and again: " But stay in the city until you are invested with the power from on high " (Lk. 24:49). In Jesus' farewell address to his apostles in the gospel of John, it is written, " When the Counselor comes from the Father, he will bear witness to me, and you also will bear witness, because you have been with me from the beginning " (15:26). It is only natural to compare these words determining the history of the church with what is reported to us in the *other writings of the New Testament.* We have already noted such harmony with the sayings of Jesus in the gospel of Luke. Differences in both composition and arrangement demonstrate that the evangelists were not concerned with a precise literal report of Jesus' words, but with the essence of his message. This becomes even more clear if we read of the missionary task which was bestowed upon the apostles in the gospel according to Matthew. Here the last message of Jesus is described as having been given on a mountainside in Galilee, but the thought behind and the concern manifest in his words agree, in spite of apparent verbal discrepancies, with the same message as contained in the Acts of the Apostles. The same is true of the promise of the Holy Spirit as reported in Matthew, when our Lord says, " Behold, I am with you all days, even to the consummation of the world " (28: 29). The comparison precisely of these two passages affords us an instructive example how in the apostolic proclamation, the sayings of Jesus are transmitted and diffused freely and with unbiased interpretation.

THE ASCENSION INTO HEAVEN AND THE SECOND COMING OF JESUS (1: 9–11)

⁹*And as he was saying these things, he was lifted up before their very eyes and a cloud removed him from their sight.*

This single sentence testifies to a meaningful event, expressed usually by the phrase " the ascension of our Lord." Here the ascension is presented as a sense-perceptible event. It is also spoken of in the gospel of Luke with the same kind of graphicness, although by different witnesses (Lk. 24: 50). The rest of the witnesses mentioned in the New Testament show greater restraint when they attest to this event.

How does Luke understand the ascension of our Lord? Does he see it as a self-contained event, one which is to be placed alongside the resurrection as its compliment and crown? The feast of the ascension, for which evidence can be adduced from the fourth century on, has given support from tradition to this view. Indeed, in all the gospel narratives, the ascension is closely associated with the mystery of the resurrection. Luke also recognizes this. In his report of the conversation of the Risen One with the disciples on the way to Emmaus, which can be rightly understood only as a revelation of the transfigured Lord, he writes, "Was it not necessary for Christ to suffer these things and so to enter into his glory?" (Lk. 24:26). Also in Luke 24:44–49 and especially in the Acts of the Apostles (1:1–8) there are words and instructions which can be correctly understood only if they are construed to come from the mouth of the Exalted One and of the Lord endowed with supernatural powers.

The state of exaltation which our Lord enjoyed had to be made visual and demonstrated to the apostles; this was done by means of the appearances of the Risen One. Through these, the testimony to which they gave voice and the faith which they professed are corroborated and deepened. The " ascension event " is nothing more than a manifestation of the exaltation of our Lord. At Luke's hands it received an enforced meaning, for it concludes the succession of post-paschal appearances of Jesus to his apostles. By his disappearance before their very eyes the way opens up, after the manner of a parable, for their testimony and for the beginning of the church. In itself this sense-perceptible entry of Jesus into heaven could have been linked to any of the other appearances of Jesus. However, through the fact that it was bound up so closely with the *last appearance* and with his final instructions, it received a special revelatory significance as a visual and graphic sign of the glorification and power of Jesus who had undergone passion and death and resurrection—the same Jesus who henceforth will be invisible to his community and to his apostles, who will nevertheless continue to work in his name. For now the era of the church has begun. With the coming of the Spirit it will receive its sealing. Through the encounters of Jesus with his apostles during the forty days after Easter the church received definitive, crucial, vital, essential revelations and instructions. At the same time, through this same means, the course of the church over and beyond the paschal revelations was brought into a deeper intimacy and closer harmony with the activity of Jesus while he was on earth.

¹⁰And as they were looking up into heaven as he went, behold two men stood before them in luminous garments, saying, ¹¹" You men of Galilee, why do you stand there, looking up to heaven? This Jesus who was taken up and away from you into heaven, will return to you in the same way as you have seen him going up into heaven."

Heavenly visitors whom we call " angels " usually act in scriptural events as *mediators and interpreters* of the activities of God. The evangelist too bestows upon them a special task. Their words are addressed to the apostles, who are looking up into heaven— that is, who are preoccupied with their questions and hopes, as they and their fellow members had been before Easter. We can readily understand the tension which their puzzlement and speculations had produced because of the conduct of Jesus; in this respect, the gospels furnish us with sufficient clues. In the narrative depicting the two disciples on their way to Emmaus this tension is described in all its starkness. The apostles gazing heavenward at the cloud of ascension are meant as a symbol for all of mankind, for all men who by reason of their earth-conditioned faith must from this time onward follow after Christ with eyes of faith and henceforth be heavy-hearted because their questions can be answered only in eternity.

What is the revelation that the onlookers experienced in the appearance of these heavenly visitors? It is contained in the sentence: " This Jesus . . . will return to you." Belief in the second coming of Jesus belongs unconditionally to the message

of the gospels, indeed in the letters of Paul and in the whole of
the New Testament. Now, for the first time, the words of Christ
at the time of his departure (1:8) become meaningful. Now,
for the first time, the apostles receive a consoling answer to
their question concerning the restoration of the kingdom of
Israel. For when he comes again, he who has left them will come
" from heaven," into which he is about to enter. This means,
consequently, that the kingdom of God will have arrived at its
required state of perfection when he comes again. Thus the
" ascension " of Jesus is not entirely the core of the narrative. It
is told here only to open our eyes to the truth that the Lord will
return to us from heaven. The era of the church now begins.
She is fully conscious of a Lord now risen and exalted; she now
realizes that she is to embark upon a journey at the completion
of which, freed from all affliction and need, she will eventually
encounter the Lord of majesty again, and see him face to face.

In Prayerful Expectation (1: 12–14)

[12]*Afterwards they returned to Jerusalem from the Mount called
Olivet, which is close to Jerusalem, a sabbath's journey away.*

This is the postscript which gives us the name of the place where
Jesus spoke his last words and where his " ascension " actually
took place. Mount Olivet played an important part in the Jewish
expectation of salvation because of its immediate proximity to
Jerusalem and to the temple. The gospel narrates various vital
events in the life of Christ which have their locale on this Mount.
From the Garden of Olives Jesus pronounced his judgment of
Jerusalem and unfolded the events preceding the end of history

(Mk. 13:3). On the same occasion he uttered this prophecy: "Then they will see the Son of man coming on a cloud with great power and majesty" (Mk. 13:26)—hence that passage which recalls the message which the angels of the ascension proclaimed.

The road to Jerusalem was short. Was it a source of pleasure to the author to offer us this precise data, which caused him to reckon the distance from the city "as one of a sabbath's journey" away? In reply, we must first of all say that this annotation does not prove that the day of the ascension was the sabbath. This short journey, perhaps two-thirds of a mile, has become for the church of definite importance for her own forward movement in space. Because of Christ's command, this road is covered by the apostles without delay (1:4). The church must have her beginning in Jerusalem. For Jerusalem, the symbol of the chosen people of God, must henceforth remain a symbol of the chosen people of God—even when the unfolding of historical events connected with Jerusalem will no longer clearly portray it as the actual center of Christianity.

[13] *When they reached there, they mounted the stairs to the upper room, where they had been lodging, namely Peter and John, James and Andrew, Philip and Thomas, Bartholomew and Matthew, James the son of Alphaeus and Simon the Zealot, and Judas the brother of James.*

We know nothing certain about the location of this upper room. It is only natural to think of a room with which the apostles were already familiar, in those days when in the company of Jesus they spent time in Jerusalem. We may assume that it was there that they celebrated the memorable last supper with their master. Acting on the instructions of our Lord, Peter and John had prepared the Pasch there (Lk. 22:8ff.). These are the same apostles whose names are found at the beginning of the list of the apostles. In this light we can perceive in the upper room a symbol of the historical relationship which exists between the pre-paschal and post-paschal era of the church. When it is related in the gospel that after their return from the experience of the ascension, the apostles " were regular in their attendance at the temple " (Lk. 24:53), this does not in any way contradict the assumption that the upper room, which also served as a rallying point even later during the subsequent growth of the Jerusalem community, was situated in a private house outside the temple. We may recall in this connection those passages in the Bible in which an upper room is mentioned as a place of prayerful solitude and of special revelation. In prayerful seclusion Peter himself became, in an upper room, the recipient of a revelation concerning the mission of the church to the gentiles (10:9ff.).

When he enumerates the *names of the apostles,* although he had previously submitted a list in his gospel (Lk. 6:14), Luke has a special purpose in mind. If before the Pasch the apostles were the special followers, now they are pictured as those men upon whom the Risen One had bestowed fullness of power and a definite mission and to whom he had consigned the labor of salvation in the church. From the very beginning and onward, the external organization and structure of the church are presented to us in this fashion—of that church whose essence is bound up in the unseen and can only be explained as the work of the Holy Spirit.

We may find certain minute differences when comparing this list with the earlier ones offered by the author, especially in the prominent place he accords to John, whom he here places next to Peter. This agrees with what the gospels bear witness to concerning the association of the two, and about which the Acts of the Apostles testifies. The name of the twelfth apostle is missing; the number eleven calls for the election of a replacement, Matthias (1 : 15ff.).

¹⁴*All these persevered steadfastly in prayer, together with the women and with Mary, the Mother of Jesus and his brethren.*

The *praying* community is brought repeatedly to our attention throughout the Acts of the Apostles. In it the example and the counsel of the Lord are shown in all their admirable effectiveness. That prayer offered " in his name " will be heard by the Father is assured by such a declaration (Jn. 16:23f.). The letters of Paul also testify forcibly to the power inherent in the prayer of the community.

Characteristic of Luke is the fact that he speaks of *women* as members of the praying community along with the apostles. Previously in his own gospel he had paid particular attention to the women around Jesus. The message of salvation, the " good news " of the New Testament, triumphs over traditional prejudices. Paul is also responsible for the newer appraisal, the creator of a new feminine *mystique,* notwithstanding that reserve towards and treatment of women retained by the mentality of the times in which he lived. Even more frequently will the Acts of the Apostles bear witness to the vocation and the activity of women in church and society.

That Mary, the mother of Jesus, is named specifically and separately fits in well with the special consideration Luke shows her in his gospel, especially in the narrative of the nativity.

Luke bestows upon the mother of the saviour a great dignity: hostess to a divine visitor bearing a divine message. Only in this passage is she named among those who will promote the growth of the nascent church. Mary belongs also to that group which will experience the ensuing pentecostal event. Her name stands out among those women who belong to the primitive church. Precisely by Luke's according her this position, we become acquainted with her unique activity among the chosen people of the New Testament.

Among the individual and separate statements of the gospels about the women who are a part of the passion story, we are given certain sure indications that we must not interpret the term " brethren " of Jesus as brothers in the blood sense of the term. By reason of general and universal biblical usage, based on the domestic laws of the Orient, it can be shown that the concept " brother " or " sister " can indicate numerous degrees and grades of relationships. We have good reason to believe that the brethren of Jesus were relations who even before the paschal event had professed themselves to be disciples of Jesus. Under such circumstances, would it have been impossible for relatives of Jesus to have been called and to have become apostles? The natural ties of blood and family do not establish either a priority or an obstacle for a vocation to apostleship with Jesus and as a result to " brotherhood " in the bond of faith.

The Completion of the Apostolic College (1 : 15–26)

A double concern motivates this narrative. The one is concentrated on the traitor among the apostles and seeks to throw light upon and inwardly to comprehend the obscure reasons which led to that apostasy which so profoundly rocked the early community. The second actual concern focusses upon the restoration of the order which had been upset by the defection of Judas by describing the manner in which the new apostle, his successor, was appointed. To understand the anxiety of the college and the faithful we must observe that by the choice of the twelve apostles Jesus had set up a basic ordinance for the chosen people of the new covenant (Eph. 2:20). " Built up on the foundation of the apostles and the prophets " is the rule which he lays down for the church, as this is visualized for us in John's Revelation in the description of the " twelve gates " (portals) and the " twelve cornerstones " which descend from heaven for the upbuilding of the New Jerusalem (21:12ff.). The relationship between the Old Testament with its arrangement of twelves (26:7) and the New Testament with its own similar arrangement is symbolized for us in the number twelve. At the last judgment the twelve apostles will sit upon the twelve thrones and will judge the twelve tribes of Israel (Lk. 22:28ff.; Mt. 19:26ff.). Thus to the primitive Christian community the group of twelve apostles must have appeared as an essential structure of the embryonic church, a structure which was at the same time especially meaningful in view of the reception of the Spirit in the immediate offing.

The Traitor in Retrospect (1:15–17)

¹⁵*During those days Peter arose in the midst of the brethren— the number of those persons gathered together was about 120— and said, *¹⁶*" Brothers, it was necessary that the saying of the scripture be fulfilled which the Holy Spirit foretold through the mouth of David concerning Judas who served as a guide for those who took Jesus prisoner. *¹⁷*He was numbered among us and was allotted his share in the ministry."*

It was not without reason that Peter was placed at the head of the list of the apostles, that his name led all the rest (1 : 13). From the very beginning this is also true of every other catalog of the apostles in the gospels. From its very formation he is considered as the leader of the twelve, the apostolic college. According to the unanimous statements of sacred scripture this precedence goes as far back as the express calling of Peter by Jesus. This is also taken for granted in the Acts of the Apostles when Peter is pictured as the spokesman and the leader of the brethren. Precisely through Peter we can discern that the juridical form of the church dates back to Jesus himself. Luke also indicates such an image of the church. This is apparent to all in the statistical data, the first of which is offered here in the statement of " a hundred and twenty " gathered together. It would appear that only men were present at this gathering. Should we see in this number, which is ten times twelve, a relationship to the twelve apostles? In the title *brethren* which is used in precise imitation of Jewish custom, we are given a new rendition, a new translation of the word which denotes the union of the faithful in Christ Jesus who personally called his apostles his brothers (Mt. 28 : 10). Paul advances a profound proof for this when he considers all Christians as " predestined " by God to be conformed to the image of his Son so that he might be the first born among many brethren (Rom. 8 : 29). In this sense we are given to understand who is meant when the Acts of the Apostles alludes to Jesus' brothers.

The first word employed in this memorable assembly deals with the betrayal of Jesus by Judas. From this we gather how painfully this deed weighed upon the infant church. This we already know from the gospels, even though they touch upon the events of the passion only rather curtly. Luke, however, tries to offer a psychological explanation for this incomprehensible deed. Three times—aside from a reference in the list of the apostles (6:16)—he speaks of the crime in his gospel (Lk. 22:3ff., 21ff., 47). In the present passage he attempts to explain the happening by means of *sacred scripture*. For in the words of Peter are contained the question and its answer as these were offered by the early church. In them we have an example of how the church takes pains to make her own experiences and her own personal position both tangible and intelligible by means of Old Testament revelation. The Risen One had declared, " Everything which has been written about me in the law of Moses, in the prophets and in the psalms, must be fulfilled " (Lk. 24:44). And in the story of the disciples on the way to Emmaus we read, " Beginning with Moses and then with all the prophets, he showed them what had reference to him in all the scriptures " (Lk. 24:27).

This story points up a basic procedure which the church initiates at this juncture, namely, to interpret and to understand the salvation event, Christ, in his relationship to and his conformity with sacred scripture. Frequently from here on we will meet with examples of this kind in the Acts of the Apostles. Even in Judaism and in its rabbinical method of interpreting the scriptures we can see typified for us in perceptible fashion the manner in which the primitive church *understood the scriptures* and adapted it to her own needs. The commentaries of the community of Qumran afford us in a special way visual models of this graphic form of interpretation and application of Old Testament scriptures. The Christian proclamation is also concerned —especially in its missionary encounters with Judaism—with recognizing and clarifying the message and the missionary labors of Christ in the light of the statements contained in Old Testament prophecies.

Now Peter brands Judas " as the guide for those who took Jesus prisoner." The personal recollection of the apostle here finds an outlet. The entire incident of the arrest of Jesus is preserved in all the four gospels and always in connection with Judas. In the above narrative, the addition of the phrase " one of the twelve " is unnerving and peace-shattering. What this means Peter attests to by the words which, although they are externally restrained and calm, nevertheless convey sentiments prompted by deepest suffering. " He was numbered among us and was allotted his share in the ministry." He was " numbered " among the group of the " twelve." In this description is to be found his uniqueness, the fact that he was chosen by Jesus himself.

In the words " the lot for this service," membership among the twelve in the fullest sense of the term is here paraphrased. " Service " in this connection means apostleship, the office of an apostle. It is characteristic of the testimony of the primitive church to emphasize frequently the vocation necessary for such service. In this passage our attention is directed both to the greatness and the sublimity of the gift which Judas enjoyed. For a similar reason, according to the gospel of John, Jesus joins to the prophecy of his betrayal the telling words, " Whoever receives one whom I send, receives me; whoever receives me, receives him who sent me " (Jn. 13:20).

THE DEATH OF THE TRAITOR (1:18–19)

[18]"(This man bought a field with the wages of his wickedness and falling face downward, burst into two at the waist and his bowels gushed out. [19]And it became known to all who dwelt in Jerusa-

*lem, so that the field was given the name, in their language,
Haceldama, that is the field of blood.)"*

We ask ourselves first of all: how is it that this note is found
in the discourse of Peter in which it is included? If we should
understand, as is suggested by the verse itself, that it is a pronouncement of Peter, speaking to the crowd that had assembled,
it would leave many questions unanswered. We must, however,
assume that many of these details were already known to the
people present. It would not solve the problems raised by the
situation if we should conclude that Peter, when using the word
" Haceldama " in Jerusalem, speaks of " your language " and
translates the proper noun into Greek; for all those present, even
the men of Galilee, were acquainted with the Aramaic dialect.
We should, rather, look upon this pronouncement concerning
the death of the traitor as an interpolation inserted by the author
into Peter's talk. He was compelled to do this so that the reader
of the Acts of the Apostles might better understand its content.
For in his own gospel, Luke never says a word about the fate
of the betrayer. If we should consider these verses as a literary
comment, then verses 1:16 and 1:20 would be drawn closer
together and as a result the interpretation of both these scriptural
sayings would be eased considerably.

THE APPOINTMENT OF A NEW APOSTLE (1:20-26)

[20]*" For it is written in the Book of Psalms, ' Let their dwellings
become desolate and let there be no one who will dwell in them '
(Ps. 69:26), and, ' May another take his office of superior '
(Ps. 109:8)."*

Both these passages in the psalms are the ones meant when we read that the " scripture be fulfilled " (1 : 16). Peter actually sees *foretold* in them the situation which had been brought about by the traitor: the vacancy in the college of the apostles and the necessity of appointing another to fill it. Anyone who reads both these texts in their context in the Old Testament from which they are taken becomes cognizant not only of another meaning, but also of another fact, namely, that the literal force of the first text is changed in such a way as to favor its applicability to the New Testament situation. For the original text reads, " Let their dwelling become desolate, and in their tents no one will ever dwell again." The church, guided by the Spirit, felt herself justified in making such changes and in offering a new version of the Old Testament, especially when, starting with the salvation event, she literally refers everything to Christ. We should recall this when we re-read what we have just said. The apostle Paul, whose letters contain numerous examples of this kind of scriptural interpretation, explains this method when he says, " All that has been written before has been written for our instruction so that we may have hope through the patience and the consolation offered us by the scriptures " (Rom. 15:4). He also speaks of the " pall " which hangs over the Old Testament under which Christ lies concealed (2 Cor. 3:13-16).

In the first citation from the psalms we might possibly detect a reference to the " field of blood " which is shunned by men. The description appears rather to fit the *vacancy created in the apostolic college* by the defection of Judas. In accepting such an interpretation we should not conceive the final clause in a sense which might possibly cause us to think that no one else could or should occupy the place that had been forfeited. We are concerned only with filling out the picture which delineates the isolation of the deserted place in order to bring to the attention of all the necessity of appointing a successor.

²¹'' *So from among those men who were together with us during the entire time that the Lord Jesus moved about among us* ²²*from the baptism of John down to the day on which he was taken up away from us—one must become with us a witness to his resurrection.''*

The Christian community is convinced of the urgency of appointing a new apostle. The number twelve must be rounded out again. The passage from the psalms serves to bolster the conviction. Of significance are the conditions which are laid down for the person to be chosen. He must be a " witness " in the sense in which this was explained in the last instruction of our Lord. Before all else, he must be *a witness to the resurrection.* For this is the decisive and definitive salvation event. Paul says of it, " If Christ was not raised from the dead, then our preaching is meaningless, meaningless also your faith " (1 Cor. 15:14). Anyone who proposes to bear witness to the resurrection must by reason of personal experience be acquainted also with all that had preceded it: the time during which Jesus lived as a man among men; the time which he spent among men as the bearer of salvation, attested to by God. The baptism of John is singled out as the beginning of this epoch. This is something more than a mere external terminus. It is also the first revelation of the mystery which surrounded Jesus (Lk. 3:21ff.). Between it and the salvific resurrection event there intervenes the salvific activity of Jesus, his public life. It is this life to which the gospel bears witness. All four gospels string their narrative between these two salvation events. The ability to bear witness to all this is required of the person who would validly assume the office of the apostle

who had defected. Thus from the very beginning of her existence
the church kept a close watch over the reliability and the faithfulness of her witnesses.

²³*They nominated two: Joseph called Barsabbas, with the surname the Just, and Matthias.* ²⁴*And they prayed, saying, " Lord,
you know the hearts of all, show us which of these two you have
chosen* ²⁵*as the one who should assume the task of service and
the office of apostle, from which Judas withdrew himself to go
his own way."* ²⁶*And they drew lots for them and the lot fell to
Matthias, and so he was numbered along with the other eleven
apostles.*

This narrative affords us a meaningful insight into the essence
of the church. It demonstrates the cooperation of the human
element, *man's efforts,* with divine activity, alone ultimately
decisive both for the planning and its execution. Two candidates
are presented to the apostles; from them a choice must be made.
Presumably there were others who could have fulfilled the
conditions laid down by Peter. The narrative supplies us with
no biographical details about these two, save their names. We
might be led to believe that the first candidate because of his high-
sounding titles might have enjoyed the best prospects. The one
chosen, however, was the second, of whom no details are given,
save that he was called Matthias.

    The church is fully aware of *God's dealings with men.* She
leaves the ultimate decision in his hands. The lot that is cast will
reveal to them his will. According to the cultural practices of the
temple it was an accepted custom to cast lots so that through
them God's will might become known. In the prayer which we

may hold to be the first "collect" ever uttered, the church professes her faith in his divine guidance or divine guidance in general. Is the prayer directed to God or in a special fashion to Christ? The literal meaning of the words themselves permits both interpretations. To show that it is a prayer to the Christ and not to God, we have in the petition itself the title " Lord "; " Lord, show us which of these you have chosen." Moreover, in the very first sentence of the Acts it is stated that Jesus " chose " the apostles (1 : 2). Anyone who reads the words of Peter (Acts 15 : 7) would, however, be inclined to look upon this prayer as one addressed to God after the fashion of the prayers in the Old Testament. The prayer of the community which we shall meet later on also suggests the same line of thought, namely, an appeal to God. In prayer constructed along the lines of a liturgical orison, namely, with a foundation which is a profession of faith, followed by an impetration built upon it, we manifest our belief that God has already made his choice and that he should out of his goodness condescend to make this known to us, in this instance through the casting of lots.

The Coming of the Holy Spirit (2 : 1–47)

The following narrative occupies a prominent place in the message of salvation, as Luke seeks to understand and proclaim it. The conclusion as well as the beginning of the Acts of the Apostles is orientated to this end (Lk. 24 : 48ff.). Due to his efforts the formative image of the church receives its profound and specific reason as well as its substantive delineation and expression. We shall try to understand it as Luke wishes us to understand it.

The Pentecostal Event (2 : 1–13)

THE REVELATION OF THE SPIRIT (2: 1–4)

[1]*When the days were fulfilled and Pentecost had arrived, all were together in one place.* [2]*Suddenly there came a sound from the heavens as of the rush of a violent wind and filled the whole house where they were staying.* [3]*There appeared to them tongues as of fire which parted and settled upon each of them.* [4]*And all were filled with the Holy Spirit and began to speak in strange tongues, just as the Holy Spirit granted them to speak.*

In solemn fashion Luke gives us the more memorable circumstances of the great event which took place on this day. Literally we should translate it as " when the day of Pentecost was fulfilled." In these words we can almost feel the tension of waiting which gripped the youthful community. " Not many days hence," *the baptism of the Spirit* would take place. Thus did our Lord express himself on the occasion of his last appearance to the apostles. The prophecy would be fulfilled on Pentecost, which we designate as the " fiftieth day " after Easter (precisely: after the sixteenth day of Nisan). This was one of the three great pilgrimage feasts which was celebrated along with the Pasch and the Feast of the Harvest (Feast of the Tabernacles). At the very origin of Judaic worship it was considered a harvest feast. Later it was transformed into a memorial of the revelation and of the promulgation of the Mosaic law on Mount Sinai. Whether this change had occurred before the Acts were composed, we do not know for sure. Special details and characteristics in the Judaic Sinaitic tradition can be found in this Lucan story, as they are related for us in the pentecostal narrative. It is certainly worthy of note that in a composition of Philo of Alexandria (died A.D. 40) the Sinai revelation is narrated in such a way as to show that as this event took place, it was accompanied by a supernatural rushing of wind and by mysterious tongues of fire, which were transmitted into divine words; and that when it is said that the seventy races of gentiles understood the proclamation of the law, each so understood it in the language of their respective country.

The Witnesses to the Event (2:5–13)

⁵Now there were staying in Jerusalem pious men from every nation under the sun. ⁶As the sound grew, a crowd came together and was greatly bewildered because each one heard the apostles speaking in his own language. ⁷They were amazed and filled with wonder and said, " Behold! are not all those who are speaking Galileans? ⁸How is it though that each one of us hears that language being spoken, in which we were born? ⁹Parthians and Medes and Elamites, and inhabitants of Mesopotamia, Judea and Cappadocia, Pontus and Asia, ¹⁰Phrygia and Pamphylia, Egypt and the parts of Libya about Cyrene, and visitors from Rome. ¹¹Jews and proselytes, Cretans, Arabians, we hear them proclaim the wonders of God each in our own language?" ¹²All were amazed and perplexed and they said to one another, " What does this mean?" ¹³Others, however, in mockery said, " They have had their fill of new wine."

Again we are dealing here with something more than an historically accurate picture. Theological considerations have collaborated in coining these lines. Judaism forms the backdrop for this pentecostal event. Thus we might ask whether the phrase " pious men from every nation under the sun " is actually meant to mark out those who were at one time Jews of the diaspora but who were now impelled by special messianic expectations to spend the evening of their lives in Jerusalem, awaiting the event. Or are we rather to think of them as pilgrims streaming into Jerusalem from all quarters of the globe to celebrate the Pasch? We shall not venture an answer or seek to settle the question. For the sentence not only indicates the world-wide dispersal of the Jewish people, but also serves to prepare for the long litany of people and races, and intimates the broad field of activity to which the apostles and the church were destined to be harvesters.

The list of peoples is a literary addition. It is intended to convey vividly and emphatically the multiplicity of witnesses to the pentecostal event and to demonstrate as forcibly as possible the great miracle of speech and of hearing that took place. The list is not to be checked against geographical charts or guidelines. For who would place Judea between Mesopotamia and Cappadocia? Why do we find no mention of the Jewish populations of other countries, such as Greece and Macedonia? The list which is presented to us serves the purpose of the author. We might be tempted to ask whether or not the additional phrase " Jews and proselytes " refers to all the preceding countries enumerated or only to the nation which had directly preceded, namely, Rome. In view of the interest of the Acts of the Apostles for Rome and for Roman readers we cannot reject the hypothesis that by this phrase Luke wishes to indicate that the pentecostal pilgrims from Rome brought back the Christian message to that city and that the newly formed and growing community there was from the very beginning composed of " Jewish and gentile Christians," even though these gentile Christians entered the church only after having been first proselytized by the Jews. In such an explanation, the two countries which follow, namely, "Cretans and Arabians," can be regarded simply as a continuation of the list in which by calculation the nine names of countries are each bracketed between three names of peoples, both at the beginning and at the end.

"The great wonders of God" form the content of the pentecostal sermon. It must have been a joyous "outcry of jubilant happiness," a proclamation of exultation over the salvific revelation of God, as it was imparted to the world in Christ Jesus. The first opportunity to express it had arrived, and with it the beginning of testimony to Christ and to his grace, with which the apostles had been commissioned in 1:8. It is the first public manifestation of the "power" of the Holy Spirit now permeating the church. How did the people react to it? Some were rendered speechless with amazement; others passed it off in mockery. It is not stretching the imagination too far to say that for those people to whom the hidden meaning of speech in various tongues was incomprehensible and whose minds were closed to the nuances of various tongues, the whole scene reminded them of a drunken revelry. Only those who were touched by the Spirit understood the message which was communicated to them in the language to which they were accustomed. Why did it remain so inaccessible to some? Did they lack openness of heart, a prime requisite? The mysterious working of divine grace is the key. But equally the guilt and the complicity of man are means of explanation. At the very beginning of her existence the church experienced the same phenomena as did the eternal Logos: "The light shone in the darkness and the darkness did not comprehend it" (Jn. 1:5).

Peter Interprets the Event (2:14-36)

THE FULFILLMENT OF THE PROPHETICAL PROMISE (2:14-21)

14Then Peter stood up before the eleven, raised his voice and addressed them. " Men of Judea, and all you who dwell in Jerusalem! Let me tell you this! Listen to my words! 15For these men are not drunk—as you suppose—since it is only the third hour of the day."

The mocking attitude of some of the audience, prompted by the pentecostal sermon to which they had listened, supplies the occasion for the special testimony of the apostle. *Peter* is again the spokesman of the college. The Acts of the Apostles incorporates in its narrative three of the more prominent missionary discourses of Peter: two before Jews (2:14ff.; 3:12ff.) and one before non-Jews (10:34ff.). It is certainly by plan that Luke also apportions to Paul three detailed sermons of which one was before the Jews (13:16ff.) and two before non-Jews (14:15; 17:22ff.). Very early in its history, the church's ecclesiastical tradition was careful about according " equal time " to these two outstanding figures in her missionary activity.

The pentecostal sermon of Peter bears a genuine Jewish stamp both in its form and in its thoughts. This Jewish cast is not restricted to the speeches in various tongues, but rather affords an opportunity to expand upon the fundamental message concerning the salvific activity of Christ and to voice a summons to profess belief in him. In rejecting the base charge of drunkenness Peter is able to insinuate the time of day that the event took place. By his reference to the " third hour " Peter was able to demonstrate that the apostles of Jesus were Jews faithful to the traditions of their fathers, who for ritual reasons were accustomed to abstain from spirits before the morning sacrifice. The community of which he is a part still feels itself united intimately with the synagogue.

It is not disputed that those " filled with the Spirit " might have conveyed the impression externally that they were drunk. Their speech must certainly have caused the listeners to surmise that they had imbibed not wisely but too well. Paul himself also indicates that he entertained a similar impression about these speeches in various languages when he says, " If the entire community gathers together in one place and all speak in various tongues, will not then outsiders and unbelievers say : you are out of your mind; you are mad?" (1 Cor. 14:23). And again in his Letter to the Ephesians he expresses the thought that perhaps they were drunk spiritually : " And do not get drunk with wine . . . but be filled with the Spirit and speak to one another in psalms and hymns and spiritual songs, and sing praises and make melody to the Lord in your hearts " (Eph. 5 : 18f.). So the pentecostal speech of itself demands a salvation historical interpretation and Peter seeks to express it.

¹⁶" *Rather this is what was said by the Prophet, Joel,* ¹⁷" *In the last days, God says, this will take place, I will pour out my spirit upon all flesh and your sons and your daughters shall prophesy; your young men shall see visions and your old men will dream dreams.* ¹⁸*Yes, in these days I shall pour out my spirit upon my servants and handmaids too, and they shall prophesy.* ¹⁹*And I will work miracles in the heavens above and signs on the world below, blood and fire and a cloud of smoke.* ²⁰*The sun will be turned into darkness and the moon into blood, before the day of the Lord comes, great and glorious.* ²¹*And it will happen:*

everyone who calls upon the name of the Lord shall be saved'
(Joel 3 : 1–5)."

Peter convincingly rejects the suspicion of natural drunkenness.
He is aware of another kind of intoxication which is about to
take place: a filling by the divine Spirit. Repeatedly the words
of the Old Testament prophets foretell this outpouring of the
Spirit as a special gift of salvation reserved to the end of time.
Isaiah, Ezekiel, Zechariah, and others speak of this. With special
vividness, however, *Joel* phrases these expectations in definite
terms. We see this borne out when the pentecostal sermon includes a rather lengthy excerpt from his prophecy. It is freely
rendered in the Septuagint, the Greek translation of the Old
Testament, with noteworthy minor interpolations which serve
to clarify its interpretation. It is worthwhile to read the entire
citation as a whole. In it we see an image of the Old Testament
concept of the end of the world. In it we can also detect traces
of messianic times as these are sketched for us from the viewpoint
of Judaism. The outpouring of the Spirit and the catastrophe in
the universe—this latter in the language of Judaism is known as
the " messianic travail " which will precede the coming of the
Messiah—are combined into one image in the perspective of the
Old Testament seer.

We are to understand the joining together of these dread events
both in heaven and on earth (circumstances which have nothing
at all in common with the pentecostal incident) as a harmonizing
of the expectations of the last days so frequently testified to in
New Testament times. This is manifest most clearly in the
prophecies concerning the end of the world to which Jesus himself gives utterance, especially in the first three gospels. Even
though the New Testament revelation teaches us to distinguish

between the advent of the last days and their fulfillment, none-theless the beginning and the end of these events are fused together. The last days have already begun also for the New Testament proclamation of the message. In any case we cannot entirely exclude the possibility that Peter possibly referred the prophetic words " miracles in the heavens above and signs on the world below " to the singular and curious signs of storm and fire which were noticeable on the morning of Pentecost. It is remarkable that precisely the word " sign " is interpolated here as an addition to the Old Testament text. We can, however, see a special reason for the citation of these cosmic events if we were to consider the emphasis that Peter places upon the last sentence of the prophet's utterance, " Everyone who calls upon the name of the Lord shall be saved." The entire pentecostal sermon is oriented to this message. Peter's sermon was delivered precisely in fulfillment of the prophecy, as well as because of the images of the catastrophes at the end of the world which are to be related to it.

THE SENDING OF THE SPIRIT, A SIGN OF THE EXALTATION OF JESUS CHRIST (2: 22–36)

²²" *You men of Israel, listen to these words. Jesus of Nazareth was a man accredited to you by God through mighty deeds, wonders and signs, which God performed through him in your midst—as you yourselves know—*²³*him who was betrayed according to a definite plan and according to the foreknowledge of God, you have nailed to the cross and killed by the hands of godless men.* ²⁴*God has raised him up, by putting an end to the pangs of death: for it was impossible for him to be held fast by it.*"

This new apostrophe brings in its wake a new train of thought. When the listeners are addressed as *men of Israel,* the admonition reminding them of their salvation-historical vocation and election resounds in their ears. "You are Israelites," declares Paul (Rom. 9:4), and by penning those words he sets before us the mystery of a people cherished by God and watched over with special care. Of course, it is also now true what the Apostle further records: "Not all who are descended belong by that fact to Israel" (Rom. 9:6).

After this very meaningful speech, we hear now for the first time the name of the one who had been announced in the event of Pentecost. Now the discourse of the apostle is turned into a *bold testimony of Jesus Christ* the Lord to whom the words of the prophet had pointed when he said: "who calls upon his name" in the new version of Joel. Anyone who further pursues the content of the pentecostal address with attention is conscious and becomes aware of the underlying, the supporting notion of the entire New Testament message.

Although the prophet Joel may have said that "the visions" and the "dreams" are nothing more than external expressions of the outpourings of the Spirit, they are nevertheless in the pentecostal sermon classified as prophetical speech, and this is stressed by his words "speeches in various tongues" as something specifically noteworthy, as something quite unique. As a consequence, it is not without reason that in the rendering and in the quotation of the text in verse 18 this repetition of the Old Testament text is added as a complementary note: "and they will talk in prophecy." All this is for Peter and for the first community a sign that the great and wondrous advent of the Lord is about to come to pass. The basic message of Jesus runs: the kingdom of God is at hand. His coming is announced in the

mysterious storm and in the tongues of fire in the revelation
of Pentecost, in the speechifying of the faithful touched by the
Spirit.

The " day of the Lord "—the question as to its exact date must
remain a matter of discussion—signifies the *judgment* in the
sense in which it forms a general biblical expectation for the
future. It hangs over mankind as a warning of him who is to
come. In this connotation the words of the prophet become a
summons to penance and to preparedness. And for this reason
the final or concluding phrase " call upon " the name of the
Lord is for the subject matter of the pentecostal sermon of decisive
significance. Anyone who wishes to survive the forthcoming
judgment, by being saved and being numbered among the living
in the sense in which the Bible understands it, needs the saving
grace of God.

Who is the " Lord " whose name we should invoke? Here
again we have another important example of a new meaning
being attached to an Old Testament concept. Joel, the prophet,
thought in terms derived from Old Testament ideas concerning
God and the relations and return of mankind to him. In the
sermon on the day of Pentecost, however, the name " Lord "—
a translation of the Greek *Kyrios*—receives an utterly new meaning. It accepts and recognizes the Lord in the exalted and resurrected Christ. Its reference and the relation to God indeed
remains, but by reason of the fact that God reveals himself in a
personal form, the divine majestic dominion is transferred to
the Lord Jesus. A notable process of New Testament salvation
belief is here attested to. It rests upon the knowledge of those who
were witnesses to the life of Jesus, of those who were in a special
fashion capable of bearing witness to the reality of the resurrection, of those who personally experienced the revelation of the

Spirit, as this took place for the first time on Pentecost and would constantly accompany the church on her way through the world. And to all these experiences is added, as a complement, the newly interpreted passage of the Old Testament prophet, the Old Testament passage of sacred scripture, as witness to the self-revealing God.

Peter can with reason appeal to the testimonial power of the works of Jesus. The " mighty deeds of Jesus " are " signs " for him through which God himself testifies that he was at work in Jesus of Nazareth. With this purpose being embodied in the miracles of Jesus, we are reminded of the gospel of John where repeatedly the same meaning is attributed to the revelatory nature of his works by Jesus himself, as for example : " For the works that I do bear witness of me that the Father has sent me " (Jn. 5:36). It may perhaps cause surprise that in verse 2:2 God is quoted and mentioned twice. This may have been done to clarify the statement that is there made. We can also see in this, however, the interest which pervades the entire sermon, namely, to permit God to appear as graphically as possible in all the activities of Jesus: God authenticated him, God worked his wonders through him (2:22), God had determined the death he was to die (2:23), God raised him from the dead (2:24, 32), God had exalted him (2:33), God has made him both Lord and Messiah (2:36).

Of importance is the statement concerning the passion and death of Jesus which is circumlocuted by the phrase so often employed in the New Testament message, especially in the account of the passion; namely, that *he was handed over*. This being-delivered-over of Jesus, which also includes the betrayal of Judas, took place, as Peter sought to stress, in accordance with the foreknowledge and the salvation-plan of God. In its most profound depths the death of Jesus cannot be explained as an event which results from purely human endeavors in the course of human history, no matter how we arrange the facts which can be historically corroborated. To make this meaning clear is a concern not only of the Acts of the Apostles. This message also plays an important role in the other books of the New Testament when they reiterate that with the death of Jesus " the scriptures are fulfilled " and " that it must be so " (Mt. 26:54), or when the resurrected Christ says to the apostles, " Thus it is written: the Messiah will suffer . . ." (Lk. 24:26). Paul also emphasizes the fulfillment of the scriptures in the death of Jesus and hence the source of his death in the salvific will of God (1 Cor. 15:3). In other passages the Acts of the Apostles speaks of the divine decree which is fulfilled in the death of Jesus (3:18; 17:3: 26:22).

This divine decree of salvation, to be wrought through the death of Jesus, does not cancel out *human guilt* which contributed to it. We perceive, if only faintly, a profound mystery in the encounter of the divine will with the actions of men. The guilt of the Jews, that is, essentially of the ruling class in Jerusalem, is also not erased by the fact that they handed over Jesus to the Roman officials (the godless men). As a consequence, the co-responsibility of the Jewish people for the death of Jesus is asserted repeatedly, openly, and without reservation. But it is Luke especially who repeatedly points out that the ignorance of men renders the guilt less culpable. The words of Christ on the cross: " Father, forgive them, for they do not know what they are doing," are valid also for the Acts of the Apostles. As do the passion narratives in all the gospels, so also does Peter's sermon concerning it insist most strongly on the fact that the testimony of the *resurrection* is the most meaningful event in

God's work of salvation. " God raised him from the dead "—
thus runs the message which we have already learned, and which
we will encounter over and over again in the preaching of the
infant church. The letters of Paul also make this proclamation.
There it is reckoned as *the* fundamental statement: " As Christ
was raised from the dead by the majesty of the Father . . ." reads
one of his many statements concerning the core of the message
(Rom. 6:4).

Thus in this passage, in connection with the resurrection, the
image of a *travail of death* is expropriated from the psalms (18:6;
16:3) (in the context of the Septuagint). The resurrection of
Jesus from the dead is contained in a unique figure of speech,
manifest now in this image: compared now to being born again
from the dead, a resurrection inseparable from that death which
Jesus bore, as it were, in his bosom. God himself freed him
from the " travail of death " as our text assumes, and thus makes
of him " the first-born of the dead " by bringing him back to
life again. Anyone who departing from the Septuagint searches
for a Hebrew basis for the image " travail of death " comes
upon those passages in the psalms which we have quoted regarding the image of the " bonds (or chains) of death." We might
conjecture that the twofold meaning of the one Hebrew word
led eventually to the phrase " travails of death."

[25]" *David did indeed speak in regard to him, ' I saw the Lord
always before me; for he is at my right hand, lest I be shaken.*
[26]*For this reason my heart was glad, and my tongue rejoiced and
even my flesh will rest in hope.*
[27]*For thou wilt not abandon my soul to the underworld and you
will not permit your Holy One to see decay.*

²⁸*You have made known to me the ways of life, you will fill me with gladness in your presence'* (Ps. 16:8–11).

²⁹*Men, brothers! I may speak to you freely and confidently about David, the Patriarch. He died and was buried, and his tomb is with us to this day.* ³⁰*Because he was a prophet and knew that God had sworn to him with an oath, he would raise to his throne one of his descendants,* ³¹*he foresaw and spoke of the resurrection of the Christ, that he was not abandoned to Hades, nor did his flesh see corruption.* ³²*This Jesus God raised up, and of that we are all witnesses."*

This excerpt must, as it stands, be read and understood in connection with the words of scripture and with their interpretation. It appears to digress from the theme of the pentecostal sermon. This passage as well as the preceding sentences concerning Jesus do, however, possess an intimate relationship to the *mystery of the Holy Spirit.* For how could we possibly conceive the Pentecost event without the salvific death of Christ and without his resurrection from the dead! Only because the paschal event was real can the mystery of the Spirit be adequately explained. Only in such a way can we understand the concern of the primitive church that the fundamental fact of the resurrection be made credible and sensible. Thus the message of the resurrection is principally supported (or substantiated) by the personal experience of the apostles, which was theirs by reason of their encounter with the Risen One. " You shall be witnesses to me " (1:8): this passage is chiefly quoted to prove that they were *witnesses of the resurrection* and had experienced it personally. Peter lays down as a condition for the college of the apostles, when the need arose to choose a new apostle to take the place of Judas who had defected, that an apostle must first of all be a *witness to the resurrection* (1:22). And when Paul seeks to demonstrate the veracity of the resurrection, he enumerates in succession these witnesses to whom Jesus appeared, and he emphatically makes the point that the majority of these were still alive (1 Cor. 15:6). Even in the passage with which we are dealing the decisive statement about the matter is to be found in verse 32: "This Jesus God has raised up; and we are all witnesses of this."

Yet from the very beginning, in addition to the external witnesses offered by the participants of the event, the church sought also *the testimony of the Old Testament revelation.* Such a method of proof corresponds to the Judeo-Christian thought-processes and to the needs of the first mission. In his first letter to the Corinthians Paul introduces his message of the resurrection by a creedal formula, a confession of faith, originating in the very earliest days of the church, when he states: "He was buried and arose on the third day according to the scriptures" (1 Cor. 15:4). And when in Antioch, in Pisidia, he also spoke of the resurrection of Jesus, he endeavored likewise to demonstrate the truthfulness of the event by means of its correspondence with what was written in the scriptures (13:30ff.). The *secundum scripturas* (according to the scriptures) in the liturgical *Credo* of the Church has its origin in the New Testament proclamation of the message of Christ. Consequently, it is both characteristic and significant for an understanding of salvation by the primitive community, that the pentecostal sermon undertakes to unite and to strengthen the personal witness of the apostles concerning the resurrection of Jesus by proof drawn from the words of revelation. Again—as it was in 1:20—it is a passage from the Book of Psalms which is used as its basis and this demonstrates anew and confirms again how frequently and how earnestly the infant

church consulted the voices of the Old Testament for her christological statements.

[33]" *Hence, Jesus, raised by the right hand of God, received the
promise of the Holy Spirit from the Father and has poured forth
what you yourselves see and also hear!* [34]*For David did not ascend
into heaven, for he himself says, ' The Lord said to my Lord:
Sit at my right hand,* [35]*until I humble your enemies as a stool
for your feet'* (Ps. 110:1).*"*

Peter now draws our attention from the resurrection and directs
it to the *exalted Lord*. This thought is important because of the
pentecostal event. For the sending of the Spirit, the reality of
which is testified to by the external, and hence sensory, percep-
tion of the human senses, can only be the work of the Lord seated
upon the throne of God. The phrase " raised by the right hand
of God " is in accordance with the previously quoted passage from
the psalms: "raised to his throne." Together with the entire
primitive Christian community Peter is conscious of this exaltation. The personal experience of this paschal phenomenon is a
warrant of this faith as are many other experiences—especially
the memorable departure of Jesus at the time of his ascension.
All the words of the Living One, now risen, still linger in their
ears, especially when the apostle speaks of the " promise of the
Holy Spirit " which had been fulfilled on Pentecost in such a
way that Jesus has received from the Father the Spirit and has
now distributed the same Spirit among his own. Here again
we find a passage from the psalms. Psalm 110, accepted by the
Jews themselves in a messianic sense, is joined to the image of
the Messiah mounting his throne. This image Peter applies to
Jesus. Even in the encounter of the pre-paschal Jesus with the

Scribes, this psalm played a special role, since Jesus himself applied it to the mystery of the Messiah (Mk. 12:35f.).

³⁶*" Hence, let the whole of Israel know that God has made this Jesus, Lord and Messiah, he whom you have crucified."*

With these concluding words the pentecostal sermon reaches its climax and attains its intrinsic objective. In its succinct, impressive formulation it appears to be an authoritative promulgation and definition of the church. The statement itself is prepared for and is substantiated by the preceding presentation. In it two fundamental concepts of the primitive church stand out prominently: *Jesus, the Lord,* the *Kyrios,* and *Jesus, the Messiah,* the Christ. This message is directed to the " whole house of Israel." The preceding considerations and arguments were directed and adapted to Jewish thought-processes. At the core of this pentecostal sermon, we can see the essence of early Palestinian proclamation in all its simplicity. Psalm 110, understood in a messianic sense, carries over the *Kyrios* concept from Old Testament theology into the New Testament where it becomes a proclamation of glad tidings, the " good news."

The First Community (2 : 37–47)

THE FRUIT OF THE DAY OF PENTECOST (2:37-40)

³⁷*When they heard these things, they were cut to the quick, and they said to Peter and to the rest of the apostles, " Brethren, what shall we do?"* ³⁸*And Peter said to them, " Repent and let*

each of you be baptized in the name of Jesus Christ for the for-
giveness of your sins, and you shall receive the gift of the Holy
Spirit. ³⁹*For the promise is made to you and your children, and*
to all those at a distance, whom the Lord, our God, calls to
himself." ⁴⁰*He bore testimony with still many other words and*
admonished them, " Save yourselves from this perverse genera-
tion!"

It was a sad note which Peter struck when he concluded his
sermon. " You have *crucified* him," whom God had so visibly
glorified by the resurrection and mission of the Spirit and had
raised to be *Lord and Master*. It penetrates our ear and strikes
terror in our heart, because it seems to be, or might actually be,
a bitter accusation of those who had perpetrated the act. True,
his hearers had not crucified him. But in verse 23 they were
compelled to listen to the words of condemnation: " You have
nailed to the cross and killed by the hands of godless men."
This accusation can neither be struck from the Acts of the
Apostles nor from the entire New Testament proclamation of
the " goods news." It would, however, be contrary to the meaning of these words, if by them we should arouse anti-Semitic
prejudices or feelings. We stand vis-à-vis to a religious tragedy.
The same thing could have happened to any other race or people.

Peter's words are addressed to the *whole of Israel;* they are,
in fact, an appeal. The infant church seeks to win the chosen
community of the Old Testament history for the message of
salvation, proclaimed by Christ. What would have happened
had the synagogue, which had rejected the invitation of Jesus,
opened itself to the pentecostal witness of the infant church,
which had matured in the womb of Judaism? We are dealing
with salvation, with the realization of what Joel, the prophet,

and with him Old Testament prophecy itself, had foretold. For Peter had toyed with this thought when he said, " For the promise is made to you and to your children." This is said for the benefit of Israel. But not without reason is that other phrase " all those at a distance " joined to the words of Isaiah. Even though we let the precise interpretation of this passage, as it is used here, remain open, we can see in it the advent of the people of God, composed as it is of all the people upon earth —a thought which is typified in symbol in the pentecostal image of all peoples.

The way to salvation, which Peter knows—and which from then on the church will know for all time—is to turn to Christ Jesus, the *Kyrios,* which even John in the desert preached (Mt. 3:2), and which Jesus himself (Mt. 4:17) had raised to the status of a preliminary preparation and condition for the coming of the kingdom of heaven; and it has now received and has been given a special relationship to the exalted Lord through the paschal and pentecostal revelation. This conversion, this summons to penance, signified the renunciation of one's previous way of life and a believing acceptance of Jesus Christ. And this will be accomplished in the mystery of " baptism " in the name of Jesus Christ, according to the economy of salvation which was formulated by him. Through it will take place everything which John the Baptist had foretold as the gift of the one who would come after him, when the time arrived for him to proclaim the " good news ": " I baptize you with water, but there is one who will baptize with the Holy Spirit " (Mk. 1:8). The " Holy Spirit " to whom testimony had been borne before the whole world in the pentecostal event will be imparted to those who confess their faith and awaken an act of hope in Jesus. Now there will be fulfilled what Peter had quoted from Joel, the prophet: "Everyone who calls upon the name of Jesus will be saved."

A Picture of the First Community (2:41–47)

⁴¹Those who accepted his word were baptized and there were added on that day some three thousand souls. ⁴²They persevered in the teaching of the apostles, remained steadfast to the community, to the breaking of the bread, and to prayers. ⁴³Each one was seized upon by fear, as many miracles and wonders were worked by the apostles. ⁴⁴All those who found their way to the faith were united and held everything in common. ⁴⁵They sold their possessions and goods and distributed them to everyone, each according to need. ⁴⁶Daily they persevered in coming together in the temple, broke bread at home, and partook of their food in joy and simplicity of heart. ⁴⁷They praised God and enjoyed the good-will of all the people. Daily the Lord increased the number of those who found the way to salvation.

By reason of Pentecost and its revelation of the Spirit, the church of Christ occupies a special place in history. It projects back into the past to the will and the labors of Christ. But it is only by the testimony of the Spirit—to which the Risen One has referred so insistently—that for the first time she adopts a course of action which shows us the *new people of God*. Luke is able to report that 3,000 people were baptized as the result of the pentecostal revelation. He is especially fond of recounting such minutiae. We assume that this is a round figure which makes graphic the great success and the progress of the primitive ecclesial mission.

The word "persevere" is here used twice (2:42 and 2:46). On four different occasions in the life of the ecclesial community it is employed: " They persevered in the teaching of the apostles, and they remained steadfast to the community, to the breaking of the bread, and to prayers."

The *teaching of the apostles* embraces the whole of the proclamation with which they were commissioned. The fulfillment of their proclamation was to be found both in the propagation of the faith and in instruction to members of the community. It was the time in which the apostolic kerygma, as we are accustomed to designate the apostolic proclamation of " good news," objectified the testimonies and the interpretations of Christ, as these were to be later incorporated in the written word of the gospels. The Christological interpretations and exegesis of the Old Testament revelation, of which we have already spoken, were further expanded and enriched in the "teachings of the apostles."

The concept of " community " is so all-embracive as to defy any definitive formulation. Some take the word to mean a " genus " under which affinite statements concerning " the breaking of bread and prayers " may be subordinated, in the manner of " species." For our part, we are inclined to think that community is an expression with a content all its own: a reference to a unique way of life, the way of life of a community, in which the faithful find themselves together through their common renunciation of all private property and the fraternal solicitude which they evidence for one another, and also through the breaking of the bread which they mutually partake of with sentiments of joy. This will be expressed more fully in the following sentences (2:44f.).

Let us pause a moment at this juncture to meditate upon the picture that is presented to us. Without anything resembling external pressure, with full freedom inherent in a personal decision, the faithful on their own initiative renounce all private property. This is stressed with even greater force in the subsequent story of Ananias and Saphira (5:4). We ought also to compare this passage with another similar narrative, namely, 4:32–37. By this comparison we can readily conclude that this renunciation took place with the greatest willingness and with joyous good-will. By this it becomes impossible to equate the attitude and the behavior of the infant Christian community with the rejection of private property in favor of a central property administration as was practiced in the community bearing the Essene stamp, the group at Qumran. Our narrative intends to give us an extremely graphic evidence of the revolution, the fundamental change in the infant church, so as to achieve the complete fulfillment of the injunction of brotherly love, as the fundamental precept which Jesus had bequeathed to them as a precious and sacrosanct duty.

The breaking of bread is a special feature of the fraternal community. " Daily . . . they broke bread at home and partook of their food in joy and simplicity of heart " (2:46). Bread as the basic food of mankind includes in its comprehension, at least in biblical usage, all other forms of nourishment. In the petition for bread in the Lord's prayer, this feature is emphatically stressed. In accordance with Jewish custom a meal began with a ritual blessing, in a breaking of bread, and so they were accustomed to designate an entire meal as " the breaking of bread." Jesus himself observed this custom at the multiplication of the loaves and the fishes (Mt. 14:19; 15:36), and at the meal he took at Emmaus, together with the two disciples (Lk. 24:30, 35). When during the celebration of the solemn last supper, before his passion and death, he mysteriously relates the breaking of bread with his death, the concept " breaking of bread " receives progressively an ever greater and more intimate relationship with the eucharistic Lord's Supper.

Did Luke think here of the cultural celebration of the Eucharist? It is not certain. Verse 46 could be given such an interpretation, though normally this special practice—" they broke bread at home "—is specifically mentioned as extra to " partaking of food." Hence we do not need to think of a daily celebration of the Eucharist. The Eucharist was actually celebrated on the first day of the week. Even when no eucharistic sacrifice was solemnly offered in connection with the meal in common the primitive community was certainly permeated by a vivid remembrance of the meal-community shared with the pre-paschal and post-paschal Jesus—and permeated also by thoughts of the second advent of Christ (1 Cor. 11 : 26). Thus in the communal " breaking of bread " the church bore striking testimony to something peculiarly her own and was initiating the decisive steps which would lead her eventually to loosen the ties which united her to the synagogue and to develop her own Christian ceremonial rites and practices.

Finally : " They partook of their food in joy and simplicity of heart." The Greek word for " joy " signifies not only an interior sentiment of " cheerfulness," but also and more specifically a " sentiment of jubilation," bursting outwardly as Paul expressed it : " We experience a sentiment of rejoicing, possessing as we do the hope of sharing the majesty of God. More than that, we rejoice in our sufferings " (Rom. 5 : 2). It is a state of heart which a human being can perceive when he frees himself from things earthly—a thought expressed so sagaciously by the Macedonians : " Despite many dreadful experiences your joy was exceedingly great and in the depths of your poverty you have shown yourselves wealthy by your exceedingly great liberality "

(2 Cor. 8:2). We should read the Epistle to the Philippians in order to become acquainted with the states of rejoicing which are the inevitable gifts of the being redeemed, and are its basic possession.

Most intimately connected with this happiness is what Luke has in mind when he uses the words " simplicity of heart." We could also translate it by " innocence of heart," if the word " innocence " did not awaken some such thoughts as " naïveté " or " indecision." By it we mean, however, that attitude which renders the individual fully accessible to God and finds in that accessibility that unique self-realization and at the same time that beatifying solitude which surpasses all understanding. We may recall here the promise made in the Sermon on the Mount : " Blessed are the clean of heart, for they shall see God " (Mt. 5:8f.). Wherever " being hidden in God " through Jesus Christ embraces the individual and mankind as a whole, " being like Christ " (or being a Christian) means being impregnated with joyousness and trust. The community (or those we have just described) possesses at the same time that power to attract, which Luke pictures when he speaks of " enjoying the good-will of the people " and of " the daily increase in the number of the faithful " (2:47).

The Activity of the Holy Spirit through the Apostles (3:1—5:42)

The Healing Powers of the Name of Jesus (3:1-26)

Of the " many signs and miracles " which were wrought by " apostles " (2:43), one is presented to us in great detail in accordance with the literary genre of the Acts of the Apostles. As in the case of Jesus himself, so in the case of the church, the miracles of the apostles are closely allied with her message. The apostles' activities are a witness by which they fulfill the task entrusted to them by the Risen One. These activities are performed not for themselves alone, but simply to serve as the occasion for and make graphic the word of the Exalted Lord.

THE MIRACLE OF THE MAN BORN LAME (3:1-10)

¹At the ninth hour Peter and John were going up to the temple to pray. ²A certain man who had been lame from birth was carried by in a stretcher; daily he was set down near the Beautiful Gate of the temple to beg alms of those visiting the temple. ³When he saw Peter and John about to enter the temple enclosure, he besought alms from them. ⁴Peter together with John looked at him and said, " Look at us." ⁵He raised his eyes to them and expected to receive something from them.

The " ninth hour " was the time set for the official service in the temple. Twice in the course of the day, once in the morning and once again in the evening, the people came together in the temple to pray and to offer sacrifice. In their own private lives the people were accustomed to devote themselves to pray thrice daily. In our own liturgical life a remembrance of this custom is still preserved. It is in harmony with the essence and with the interests of a religiously established community that its members gather together in common at suitable times to acknowledge by prayer their profession of faith in God; by so doing, their private prayer and their personal devotions are in no way interfered with, but rather are fostered.

Prayer and almsgiving have always been allied as fundamental activities of men animated by religion. The Sermon on the Mount (Mt. 6: 1ff.) and many passages in the gospel bear witness to this practice. A beggar might reasonably assume that where people pray together, heart and hands would be more readily inclined to relieve the *needs of the poor*. The man at the gate was poor not only because of his apparent poverty, but chiefly because of his lameness, inherited at birth and considered incurable. In the persons of Peter and John, the church encounters human need. The pleading gestures, the hopeful gaze, implore help in the form of what is nearest at hand, especially what is easiest and least painful, what humans are accustomed to give to one in distress; small change, coins of various denominations.

⁶Peter, however, said, " Silver and gold I do not have, but what I have, that I give you. In the name of Jesus of Nazareth, rise and walk!" ⁷And he took him by the right hand and raised him up. Then suddenly power flowed into his feet and bones. ⁸He jumped up, he was able to stand erect and to walk; and he accompanied them into the temple, running and leaping and praising the Lord.

If Peter and John were not able to dole out either silver or gold, their inability is not to be sought in their mean estimation of material gifts. In fact, on several occasions Jesus himself appears to have come to the aid of the poor with money (see Jn. 13:29), and Paul praised the zeal with which the Christians of Macedonia contributed to the collections for the poor of Jerusalem and by their example encourage the Corinthians to donate generously of their worldly goods (2 Cor. 8:1ff.). When Peter speaks of gold and silver, which represent large sums of money and hence scarcely ever would be given as gifts to beggars, he alludes to that gift which can never be compared with silver and gold—*curing of the sick*. From what source had he derived such knowledge? Frequently he had co-experienced how Jesus had healed the sick by the power of his word. This Jesus has, however, entered into the glory and the majesty of his Father; but he is present in the Holy Spirit whom he had made visual on the day of Pentecost. Only by reason of this mysterious presence—as we shall see more clearly later on—could Peter have had a presentiment of or have faith in his own personal possession of such a gift, the power to cure. It would not make much sense if we attempted to explain the entire event by means of natural reason alone.

" In the name of Jesus of Nazareth, rise and walk." What wealth of meaning is contained in these simple words: Peter knew of the *exaltation of Jesus* to the right hand of the Father. In the sermon on Pentecost he had stated this very clearly. But in this passage he still mentions him as if he were still here upon earth, because when he speaks of Jesus now he goes so far as to name his home city, Nazareth. He is strictly conscious of the nearness of Jesus, the exalted *Kyrios*. In his last words the Risen One had promised to his own, " You will receive power " (1:8). " Behold I am with you all days even to the consummation of the world " was his last promise to the disciples (Mt. 28:20). And in Mark, this same conviction of the church is similarly expressed: " These will support as signs those who believe: in my name they shall cast out devils; they shall speak new languages; they shall pick up serpents; and if they should drink anything deadly, it shall not harm them. They shall lay their hands upon the sick, and these shall become well again " (16:17ff.). Among the gifts of the Spirit, Paul enumerates the following: " the gift of healing " and the " gift of working miracles " (1 Cor. 12:9).

⁹All the people saw him walking and praised God, ¹⁰and when they recognized him as the one who sat daily at the Beautiful Gate of the temple begging for alms, they were filled with wonder and amazement at what had happened to him.

The miracle stimulated *excitement* and caused the people to ask *questions*. We know of similar incidents of this kind from the gospels. Again and again we read statements such as the following: " And they were worked up and they praised God and were filled with fear, and they said: ' We have seen strange things today' " (Lk. 5:26). This wonderment is fully in accord not only with the usual style of a narrative of the miraculous, but also is conditioned and made comprehensible by psychological considerations. Let us consider the situation as it was. The man cured of his lameness was forty years old (4:22). For decades he must have always occupied the same place; for the ordinary visitor of the temple he actually formed a part of the accustomed image of the beautiful gate. Would it not have caused wonderment and amazement when they saw him leaping about and praising God? We can consider this event as authentic, genuine history. The extraordinary and the mystifying do not compel us to think of it as a pious legend which the author could have invented for his own use in the proclamation of the faith.

THE CURE , A SIGN OF THE RISEN ONE (3:11–16)

¹¹While he clung to Peter and John, all the people rushed to

them in the porch of Solomon, and they were beside themselves.
¹²When he noticed this, Peter addressed the people, "Men of
Israel! Why are you so astonished over this or why do you stare
at us, as if we had by our own hands or piety brought about
that which had caused him to walk?"

The miracle affords us an opportunity to meditate for a moment
on the *revealing word.* As we saw this word at work during the
incident on Pentecost, so we meet it in the gospels. An external
event and an explanatory word are brought together to make
visible the advent of salvation. The scene unfolds in the portico
of Solomon, in the hall-like arrangement dating back to the
temple of Solomon, on the eastern perimeter of the temple area.
This locale has for the infant community a special tradition
behind it. In this very same hall Jesus himself had preached to
the people (Jn. 10:23), and according to the Acts of the Apostles
the group of disciples was accustomed to meet there regularly
(5:12). Here we can perceive the beginnings of what would
become unique for the Christian community, but within the
outer framework of Jewish practice and rite.

Peter addresses the people a second time. It is again a speech
peculiarly suited to Jewish mentality and to Jewish thought-
processes. The event itself is a testimonial to the salvific activity
of God in Christ, and likewise a summons to repentance and to
faith. And again an appeal is made to the *testimony of scripture*
to substantiate the salvation event. The proof that the " good
news," the glad tidings, enjoy an intimate relationship to the
Old Testament revelation was indeed, as we have seen previously, a pressing concern of the apostles' proclamation. First of
all, Peter brushes aside—as this is a commonplace as well as a
characteristic of the Lucan narrative—a misunderstanding which

might be present. And later on both Barnabas and Paul also take pains to ward off an erroneous interpretation of the miraculous healing of the man born lame in Lystra (14 : 9f.).

What does Peter say? First of all, he refuses to ascribe to himself anything which might prevent the people from learning that what was done was of divine origin, although what struck their eyes might have seemed otherwise. Ocular evidence cannot always be relied upon. He impugns the possession of *personal power,* such as Simon the magician sought to attribute to himself (8 : 9ff.). He also rejects as false any claim that the miracle might have been wrought because of the piety of both John and himself. What does he mean by that? Does he wish to bracket out prayer or the power of prayer? Does he not know what Jesus had promised those who pray, " Ask and it will be given to you " (Lk. 11 : 9)? Was he ignorant of the meaning of that majestically comforting phrase, " Whatever you ask the Father, that he will give you in my name " (Jn. 16 : 23).

Peter is certainly aware of the power of prayerful faith. He knows that in this very cure such a prayer was intimately interwoven. In this situation, however, he is so deeply concerned with bearing witness to the *activity of God* that he seeks to repress everything which might give the appearance that the miracle was performed because of his own personal merit. Here we encounter an attitude which considerably enhances the image of the one burdened with the task of preaching the message of salvation. Free of all selfishness, liberated from all egocentricity, Peter ascribes the miracle to the testimony with which he is entrusted. His human mediatorship is relegated to the background in favor of the activity of the Spirit whom he serves.

13" *The God of Abraham and of Isaac and of Jacob, the God of*

our fathers has glorified his servant Jesus, him whom you de-
livered up and disowned before Pilate, when he had resolved to
set him free. ¹⁴*You have disowned this holy and just one and*
demanded that a murderer be the recipient of your mercy. ¹⁵*You*
have killed the author of life, whom God raised from the dead.
Of this we are witnesses. ¹⁶*Thanks to faith in his name, by this*
same name he has bestowed strength upon this man whom you
see and know, and this faith, moreover, working through Jesus
has conferred upon him perfect health before your very eyes."

Peter places the miracle of healing under the light of the self-
revealing God. In a moving salvation-historical vision he directs
the gaze of all to the salvation event of God in Christ Jesus.
Those who read the account with care will experience the broad
sweep and the profound depth of his statement. It is an awesome
summons to Jewish reasoning, a compelling appeal to their
religious conscience. *The God of Abraham, of Isaac, and of
Jacob* is the " God of your fathers." With deliberate forethought
the title of God is chosen and employed. It is familiar to Jews
and to Jewish speech and is full of profound meaning. It
awakens thoughts of Moses, who was the first to have learned
this title of God, when God spoke thus to him: " This shall be
my name forever and this my name from generation to generation " (Ex. 3:15). The presence of salvation is typified and pre-
figured in Moses—the saviour of his people, called by God;
in him the salvific figure of Jesus is made manifest, as the testimony of the New Testament bears out and as the Acts of the
Apostles specifically attests to.

God glorifies *his servant Jesus.* Even in the prayer of the
community Jesus is addressed as " the holy servant of God "
(4:27). The words of Isaiah which Matthew cites in reference

to Jesus come to mind: "Behold the servant, whom I have chosen, my beloved, with whom my soul is well pleased. I will put my spirit upon him, and he will proclaim justice to the peoples . . . and the peoples will place their hope in his name" (Is. 42:1ff.). It can scarcely be doubted that Peter's sermon intends to point to the "servant of God," endowed with ever new lineaments by Isaiah, and so he completes the equation, so surprising to the Jewish mentality, to the effect that this servant of God has appeared in Jesus.

When Peter used the words "You have disowned this holy and just One," did he also think of *his own denial*? At the time he spoke, he knew and acknowledged his own guilt. He speaks as one of the wicked, when in his introduction he speaks of "the God of our fathers." Oneness with his people and the knowledge of his own guilt give him the right to speak so openly and so freely of his own personal guilt in the sight of Christ. Again we are brought into contact with the tragedy of the human person, of which we are reminded as often as the name of Pilate is named (see 4:27; 13:28).

But it is not for the sake of accusation that the failure of human beings in human affairs is so sharply highlighted; rather, Peter was concerned—as he was in the sermon on Pentecost day —with *the testimony of God's salvation event* in Jesus Christ. The essential and substantive message of his words is thus found in the words: "whom God raised from the dead. Of this we are witnesses."

On this occasion Peter is compelled to speak of the *resurrection of Jesus*. This is not only the testimony of God to his "servant" Jesus and hence a fitting confirmation of his mission: this is not only the "glorification" of the "author of life," abandoned by men; it is also the true reason for the *miraculous cure of the man born lame.* This is attested to in a statement which is both somewhat cumbersome and intellectually demanding and consequently so meaningful for the purpose for which it was used (3:16). Twice the notions " faith " and " name " appear in the sentence. The decisive reason for this, then, should be understood, but this can be achieved only after some meditation. The healing is not the result of a purely human action; it was performed by " a servant " whom God had raised and glorified. Jesus' " name " had raised a man, who was born lame. Peter himself had bestowed this prodigy upon " the name of Jesus." This name embraces the entire mystery of the Lord Jesus: his essence and his power. The power of this " name " paved the way to the " faith " which enables us to make a profession of faith in, and trustfully acknowledge, Christ's nearness; for this faith is made real and workable through the spirit of Christ who is given us. There is a mystery about this faith: it appears to be nothing more than a human act, that is, one originating with and in man, whereas it is also a gift of the Holy Spirit (1 Cor. 12:9).

We may again ask ourselves another question: *whose faith* did Peter have in mind? Certainly that faith by which he was enabled to pronounce the words of the cure! The text says nothing at all of what took place in the lame man. He expected, no doubt, nothing more than the customary alms. Or was there awakened in him, by the mere touch of the hand of the apostle and by his words, all that was necessary to evoke a spontaneous act of faith? We are faced here with an interior encounter of man with God. We can only guess at what the man had actually experienced. By speaking so powerfully of the power of the name of Jesus and of faith in him, and by impressing these truths so emphatically and thoroughly upon the lame man, Peter adopts a procedure by which he was able to lead the astonished people (the ocular witnesses) from their initial astonishment to a salvation-effective faith.

REPENTANCE AND FAITH (3:17–26)

[17]*"And now, brothers, I know you acted out of ignorance as did also your leaders:* [18]*But in this way God permitted to be fulfilled what has been foretold through the mouths of all the prophets, that his Christ should suffer."*

" Father, forgive them, for they know not what they do," Jesus prayed as he hung dying on the cross. These words, here recalled by Peter, are directed to the Jewish people because of the title with which he addresses them, namely, *brothers.* Peter also attributes the mitigating factor of ignorance to the leaders of the people. Paul expresses this same thought when, in the synagogue at Antioch, in Pisidia, he cries out to his Jewish audience, " Those who lived in Jerusalem and their rulers did not recognize him and by so doing fulfilled through their condemnation of him the sayings of the prophet " (13:27). And in his first letter to the Corinthians he says, " We proclaim the wisdom of God, mysterious, hidden, which God predestined for our glorification before the world's beginning. Not one of the rulers of the people in this world recognized it: for had they recognized it, they would not have crucified the Lord of glory as they did " (1 Cor. 2:7).

With what kind of recognition are we dealing? Actually, according to all, with that recognition of the *divine mystery of Christ,* with the recognition of his mission, originating in God. This admission of ignorance does not cancel out man's share of blame in the death of Christ; and the preceding statement retains all its force: "You have murdered the author of life." As we have already seen, this was first said in the sermon on Pentecost (2:23, 36), and will frequently recur later on in the Acts of the Apostles.

Nevertheless—as was the case in the sermon on Pentecost—the acknowledgment of human guilt is linked to the *testimony of the divine decree,* which was fulfilled in the *passion of Christ.* The foretelling of this prophetical revelation of God became a reality, permitted by God, in the sufferings of Christ. As we have already seen, this interpretation of the death of Jesus in a salvation-historical sense is essential to apostolic preaching. The words which Jesus spoke to his disciples on the way to Emmaus again come to mind: "Was it not necessary for Jesus to suffer these things and so enter into his glory?" (Lk. 24:26). And we encounter these same thoughts again according to Luke in the last words of the Risen One to his apostles: "Christ will suffer, and on the third day he will rise from the dead" (Lk. 24:46). In these words we perceive the struggle and the search of the infant church for reasons which would make understandable and meaningful the infamous death of Christ, which at least in the eyes of the world was so disgraceful. How necessary this was we can judge from the confession of St. Paul in his first letter to the Corinthians: "We preach Christ crucified, a stumbling block to the Jews and folly to the gentiles" (1:23).

Peter, too, experienced or sensed the scandal which Christ's suffering on the cross in so great debasement must have cast upon the concept of a Messiah, so widespread among the Jews at the time. And for this reason it was obligatory for him to meet the scandal head on by referring to the glorification of

Jesus in the resurrection, and by bringing out into the open
the fact that his death and resurrection were entirely in accord
with the scriptures. A further *sign of the Risen One* is for him
also the healing of the man born lame, which was prompted by
belief in the name of Jesus. Thus this cure and its interpretation
are inserted into the testimony for Christ in the infant community as a visual perceptible example. This can be recognized
in the sentence: " Each one was seized upon by fear, as many
miracles and wonders were worked by the apostles " (2:43).

[19]*"As a consequence repent and be converted so that your sins
may be blotted out,* [20]*and so the times of the quickening of the
Spirit may come from the presence of the Lord* [21]*and he may send
Christ Jesus predestined for you, Jesus, whom heaven must
receive, until the times for the restoration of all things which
God spoke through the mouths of his holy prophets from of
old.* [22]*Thus Moses spoke, ' The Lord, our God, will raise up
for you a prophet from among your brothers, as he did me.
You must listen to him in all things whatever he will say to you.
*[23]*But it shall, however, be so: everyone who does not listen to
this prophet shall be destroyed from among the people '* (Deut.
18:15, 19). [24]*And all the prophets who have spoken, from
Samuel's time onward and those after him, proclaimed these
days.*

Just as in the sermon on Pentecost, the admonition to repentance
is again voiced to the people present, struck as they are by the
mysterious happenings and by the words of the apostle. *Repent
and be converted,* so runs the admonition. Why does Peter not
also enumerate baptism among the signs by which salvation
can be gained? Yet baptism as an indispensable means of salvation is without doubt included in his admonition to " repent

and be converted." For reasons to be found in his presentation —because of the proximity of the pentecostal narrative—Luke possibly did not think it was necessary to mention baptism again. He is permitted to take for granted that the reader is already familiar, and in possession of, such knowledge. We are justified in understanding the narratives of the Acts of the Apostles in this sense, for frequently the evangelist chose to take similar information for granted in his gospel.

We may thus conclude that baptism is also incorporated in the promise of the forgiveness of sins. For in the New Testament message, conversion and the forgiveness of sins are inseparably connected with baptism in the name of Jesus Christ.

To the admonition to repent is joined an important notion of Jewish thought. *The times of the quickening* are held out in prospect for the people. As in the sermon on Pentecost, so also here the eschatological expectations of Judaism are appealed to; and Israel's hope for the dissolution of the present chronological order, evoked by thoughts of a better and more attractive epoch, is frequently evidenced in the earlier word-images of revelation. Because of their bewitching, alluring visions, the prophets announced the happiness to be found in this era of salvation, and at the same time juxtaposed it against strict, austere, harsh summons to repentance and conversion. It is this expectation of Judaism which Peter alludes to when he combines the " times of quickening " with his summons to change of heart and repentance. His own specific concern, however, is directed to linking this eschatological hope to that One who by his passion and resurrection and finally through the revelation of his Spirit was singled out by God as the authentic and unique mediator of salvation. The healing of the man born lame was also fitted into this revelation as a sign of the " glorified servant of God."

Consequently, man's change of heart and the conversion of mankind are to be concentrated on Jesus Christ. The remission of sins will be obtained through him. We are reminded of a passage in Peter's second letter: " How very holy and pious lives ought you to lead as you await and hasten the coming of the day of the Lord " (2 Pet. 3:11). Salvation will be accomplished in the " days of the quickening " only when the people have made themselves ready for it. A profound law of salvation is thus promulgated. We are admonished here about the mysterious relationship which exists between *man and creation,* as Paul points out when he says, " All creation awaits with eager longing for the revelation of the sons of God. For creation itself would be freed from slavery to corruption to enjoy the freedom of the children of God " (Rom. 8:19f.). The Revelation of John further supports this view in its description of a heavenly Jerusalem.

Jesus Christ will, therefore, at the *restoration of all things,* come again from heaven. This denoted the embodiment of the Majesty of God and for the moment the state and place which has swallowed him up. Yet what precisely does the notion of " restoration " actually mean? We can translate it either as the " restoration of all things " or " the restoration of the universe." The meaning of the sentence is certainly not that Jesus must, as it were, " wait " until " everything of which God had from of old spoken through the mouths of the prophets " finds its fulfillment. It signifies rather the final condition of all things when the world has reached its goal, as this is portrayed for us in the parable of the cockles at harvest time (Mt. 13:39) or in the sermon on the end of the world preached by Jesus, when the apostles asked him, " What is the sign to herald your coming and for the consummation of the world?" (Mt. 24:3). We may also recall these words of the Risen One: "Behold, I am with you until the consummation of the world" (Mt. 28:20).

"The times of the quickening" and "the restoration of all things" are—so Peter seeks to say in accordance with the literal meaning of the words—in the decrees of God connected with man's readiness and openness for salvation. The apostle directs his talk first of all to the Jewish people. He foresees the arrival of the new Moses in the person of Jesus Christ. The saying so treasured for so long a time by the Jews, namely, that there will come a *prophet of the future* (Deut. 18:15), is in Peter's words fulfilled in Jesus Christ. The salvation or the damnation of mankind will be determined by him. Already in the gospel there is an allusion to the word of Moses, when the Jewish delegation posed the question to John the Baptist, "Are you a prophet?" (Jn. 1:21), or when in still other passages the amazed populace time after time recognized and expressed their realization that Jesus was indeed a prophet.

[25]" *You are the sons of the prophets and of the covenant which God has entered into with your fathers, when he spoke to Abraham, ' In your seed all the generations of the earth shall be blessed* ' (Gen. 22:18). [26]*For you, first of all, God raised up his servant and sent him to bless you so that each one of you might repent of your wicked deeds.*"

In accordance with the Hebrew literary genre Peter turns to the " sons of the prophets and of the covenant which God had entered into with your fathers." The " God of Abraham, Isaac, and Jacob " and " the God of your fathers " are made synonymous with God who has " glorified " his servant Jesus. " What he had promised to their fathers," he must now fulfill in the *persons of their sons,* the people of Israel. The promised blessing will be imparted and shared by all who welcome him in faith, namely, Jesus, " the seed of Abraham." In the quoted passage from sacred scripture, Genesis 22:18, we are vividly reminded of thoughts found in the letters to the Romans and to the Galatians, where Paul takes pains to explain the meaning of sonship for the new seed of Abraham, in order to show that in Jesus Christ, promised to Abraham, the blessing to come is realized.

What is the " content " of this " blessing "? Peter tells us: " that each of you might repent of your wicked deeds." Is that all? Does this not sound somewhat disillusioning? But as the subsequent text suggests, the sermon of the apostle was terminated by the intervention of the authorities. Even if it did appear to be abruptly concluded, there is still great significance to be attached to this verse. Did not the sermon on Pentecost end with blunt, harsh words (2:36)? *" Repent of your sins and of your wicked deeds "* is the primary and most significant concern of the " good news " which concluded Peter's words at that time. Did not the apostle begin his sermon with a summons to a change of heart and to repentance? And did he not promise that " the times of the quickening of the Spirit may come from the presence of the Lord and he may send Christ Jesus predestined for you "? Is this not blessing enough? This is the embodiment and fulfillment of the blessing. Truly it affords a sufficient motive for the people to repent of their wicked deeds.

Finally, we should not pass over the words " first of all " without assigning to them the value which is their due. " For you, first of all, God raised up his servant and sent him to bless you." The historical vocation of Israel—which all the New Testament writings reveal knowledge of—is here appealed to. Paul is only too well aware of the pre-eminence of the chosen people. He also knows of their denial and tries to the best of his ability to make them understand what they did by the strongest arguments he can muster (especially in Romans 9–11). With Peter's sermon the mission to the Jewish people begins. The church will attempt, while maintaining contact with the Jewish community, to win the Jews to belief in him to whom not only the voice of the past bears witness, but whom God himself had since singled out and glorified as the Expected One. In the " first of all " it is also impressed upon us that *not the Jews alone* had been offered salvation, as Judaism had so widely believed. The chance to decide for themselves whether or not to accept salvation had been offered to the Jews *first of all* among all the people in the world —due to their special place in the economy of salvation. Likewise in his first mission sermon Paul thus addresses the synagogue of Antioch, in Pisidia: " It was of necessity that the word of God be proclaimed first to you. Since you reject it and judge yourselves unworthy of eternal life, behold now we turn to the gentiles " (13:46).

The Testimony of the Sanhedrin (4:1–31)

THE ARREST OF THE APOSTLES (4:1–4)

¹*While they were speaking to the people, the priests, the captain of the temple, and the Sadducees approached them, ²annoyed because they were teaching the people and proclaiming the resurrection of the dead in the person of Jesus. ³They arrested Peter and John and placed them in custody until the next day; for it was already evening. ⁴Many, however, of those who had listened*

*to the word became believers and the number of faithful rose to
about five thousand.*

We know of the hostile tension which had developed between
Jesus and the Jewish authorities by reason both of his message
and his activity; we know, too, of the passionate and emotional
struggle he had with the priestly officials which eventually ended
in his death on the cross. In unmistakable language Jesus had
also prophesied that hatred and persecution would be the lot of
his chosen ones, and in this way he prepared them for it. In his
eschatological sermon as found in the gospel of Luke, Jesus told
his disciples, " But before all these things happen, they will lay
their hands on you and persecute you; they will deliver you to
synagogues and prisons and drag you before kings for my name's
sake " (Lk. 21 : 12f.).

Anyone who reads the farewell address of Jesus in the gospel
of John encounters the prophecy concerning *the hatred of the
world,* bolstered by an even more cogent argument: " If the
world hates you, bear in mind that they hated me before you. If
you were of this world, the world would show its love for its
own : because you are not of the world, since I have singled you
out of the world, for this reason the world hates you . . . You
will be thrown out of the synagogues; yes, the hour is coming
when whoever kills you, will believe that he has offered a sacrifice to God " (Jn. 15 : 18ff.). In the Johannine sermons, however,
we also meet up with the strongest and most convincing allusions
to the aid of the Paraclete, the Holy Spirit, during the forthcoming persecutions.

The prophecy of Jesus was soon fulfilled. It would have been
odd had it been otherwise. The legal process employed against
Jesus lay in the not too distant past; the dust of history had not

as yet settled. The same persons who had condemned him were still considered as *rulers of the people*. Now the people, insofar as they had not been led astray by their political or religious leaders, were stirred by and thankful for the " good news " and held the community in reverential awe. The rulers, however, were animated by hatred and jealousy: as they had been in the past in their struggle with Jesus, so now they were again filled with the same emotions in the persecution of the church.

Along with the priests our text mentions the temple captain and the Sadducees, the authoritative officials of the temple. The Sadducees, who differed in many respects from the more eminent Pharisees, nonetheless played a major and a more decisive role in the trial of Jesus. The high priest and his colleagues formed a closely knit group of conspirators. We will meet them again in the trial in which they had involved Paul (23: 1ff.). What gave them the excuse to proceed against Peter and John? Without doubt they were enraged by the huge crowds of people who were attracted to them. As the subsequent narrative attests, the problem of the cure of the man born lame was supposedly the primary charge in the investigation. But the text almost makes it quite clear that for a long time they had been scandalized by the public appearances of the apostles and their propagandizing preaching on behalf of Jesus. They were especially filled with animosity because the apostles were preaching Jesus' resurrection from the dead (4: 2f.). We know that historically the Sadducees were fundamentally opposed to the resurrection of the body; in this they were directly contrary to universal Jewish belief.

For the first time the apostles are thrown into prison. The course which they will follow in giving their testimony in the future is clearly depicted as is also the course of their future apostolate. Despite all this, *the church grows*. Another note-

worthy feature is presented in this narrative: alongside the fact
that Peter and John are arrested, Luke notes that because of the
sermon many who had listened went away no long unbelievers,
but believers, and that the number of the faithful rose from
three thousand on Pentecost day to five thousand on this occasion. A special motif of the Acts of the Apostles stands out in
this short notice. Despite opposition and persecution, the commission imposed by and the prophecy of the Risen Lord were
being fulfilled. In a very tangible fashion the infant church was
experiencing the power of the Holy Spirit.

Their Testimony before the Sanhedrin (4:5–12)

*⁵On the following day, as the rulers and the elders and the
Scribes were gathered together in Jerusalem ⁶along with Annas,
the high priest, and Caiaphas, John and Alexander, and all the
members of the high priest's family, ⁷they brought the apostles
before them and questioned them, " By whose power or in
whose name have you done this?" ⁸Then, filled with the Holy
Spirit, Peter said to them, " Rulers of the people and you elders!
⁹If we have been arraigned before you today to give an accounting for a benefit conferred on a sick man and concerning his
healing, ¹⁰let it be known to all of you and to all the people of
Israel: in the name of Jesus Christ, of Nazareth, whom you
have crucified, whom God however has raised from the dead;
through him this man stands before you perfectly healthy. ¹¹He
is the ' stone which rejected by you the builders has become the
corner stone ' (Ps. 118, 22). ¹²And there is salvation in no other;
since there is no other name under heaven, which might have
been conferred upon man, by which we must be saved."*

The two apostles whom we have come to know from the gospel

accounts as simple men now enter *the judgment chamber (court room) of the supreme authority* among the Jews. The rulers of the people are assembled. Not without reason does the Acts of the Apostles number the representatives of the civil groups and enumerates by name the authoritative deputies of the priestly state. Despite his deposition by the Romans, Annas is still the most influential member of the high-priestly tribe, and his son-in-law Caiaphas is the official high priest; they are already known to us from the trial of Jesus. Although the Romans, the occupation power, were deployed throughout the country, the Supreme Council still retained its position of principal authority for Judaism. Money and intelligence, culture and power are embodied in this tradition-rich body, which thanks to its close ties with worship and religion possessed both authority and esteem.

Peter was fully aware of the authority of the high priest. In the titles he used in opening his speech, he expressed the reverence which the Jewish people were accustomed to show in the presence of superiors, appointed by God. As we have already seen, the infant church felt itself bound by the social and religious regulations of Judaism. Peter's outward respect offered no obstacle to his freedom, nor did it present an obstacle to his ingenuousness in his choice of words. This is demonstrated by the manner in which he describes the character of the trial. The apostle recognizes from the very outset that he and John are being subjected to interrogation not because of a questionable deed but because of a benefit that they had conferred. Solemnly and challengingly repeating the admonitions contained in the conclusion of his address on Pentecost, Peter introduces the actual subject matter of the quizzing and of his own testimony when he boldly proclaims the message of salvation announced by Jesus Christ, and links it to the healing of the man born lame.

The man healed of his infirmity himself stands before the supreme Jewish authorities! For Peter would not have done justice to his divinely appointed task had he not employed the occasion to air the imperative message of personal and definitive salvation. He speaks frankly before the very assembly which a short while before had sentenced Jesus to death; he speaks of him and of the guilt of the gremium by joining to the name of Jesus the phrase: *whom you have crucified.* Though he had been able to speak in such terms to the people in his sermon on Pentecost, now he voices this accusation before the responsible leaders of the people. It seems that he has thrown caution to the winds.

But here there is coupled inseparably with the words concerning the crucifixion the message of resurrection wrought by God. The figure of " cornerstone "—taken from Psalm 118—characterizes the blindness and the tragedy of the chosen people.

THE HELPLESSNESS OF THE AUTHORITIES (4:13–22)

[13]When they perceived the candor of Peter and John and ascertained that these men were unlearned and uncultured, they were astonished. They did in truth recognize them as followers of Jesus [14]but they did not know at that moment what to allege against them because the lame man who had been healed was standing with them. [15]They ordered them to leave the council chamber and conferred together, saying, [16]" What shall we do with these men? All the inhabitants of Jerusalem knew that they worked a miracle, and we cannot call it into question. [17]Lest it be further spread among the people, let us impress upon them with threats not to speak any longer to anyone in this name."

The members of the Sanhedrin had to swallow their pride at these courageous words. Actually we might have expected that they would have flown into a passion and have pronounced a devastating sentence against the two apostles precisely because of the tension generated by their accusation—just as they had done in the trial of Jesus or as later actually happened in the judicial examination of Stephen (7:54ff.). What now restrained them? It was certainly, as verse 21 enunciates so clearly, the respect or the fear of the populace which was in the final analysis decisive for the course they took. We know from the gospels themselves how the Jewish officials time after time hesitated to proceed against Jesus because the mood of the people was deemed unfavorable. Public opinion has frequently been the guideline which has motivated authorities to pass sentences, be they right or wrong.

There appear, however, to have been other factors which determined the conduct of the Supreme Council. The man healed of his lameness stood alongside the apostles as an irrefutable witness to the reality of the cure. Besides, the dramatic appearance of Peter had the effect of disarming them somewhat, since both of the apostles lacked educational background and cultural attainment and because Peter, despite such handicaps, spoke so masterfully. *They did not know with what to charge them,* so runs the meaningful narrative. In their momentary extremity they seized upon a straw, they used a dodge which would, nevertheless, be frequently employed later on to smother the inspirations of the Spirit: they issued a prohibition against speaking in public. They hoped through it—and this in spite of their own misgivings—to be able to reduce them to silence, and to put an end to their testifying in the name of Jesus. In their decree, however, they could not bring themselves to use the name of Jesus (see also 5:28). In this alone they manifested their hatred and their antipathy to the Christ. He must be hushed up and bracketed out at all costs.

[18]*They summoned them back and charged them, they must not speak or teach at all in the name of Jesus.* [19]*Peter and John, however, answered them, " Whether it is right in the sight of God to obey you rather than God, you must decide for yourself,* [20]*for it is impossible for us to keep silent about what we have seen and heard."* [21]*With further threats the authorities dismissed them, because they could find no ground on which to punish them because of the people. All praised God for what had taken place.* [22]*For the man in whom the miracle was worked was more than forty years of age.*

This momentous occasion has become a model for the course over which the church has moved through history. What took place at that moment clarifies a rule which demands observance everywhere: that human law is subordinate to divine law. The apostles rejected categorically the prohibition to speak which had been laid upon them by the Sanhedrin. In the trial which will soon take place, they will express their objection even more vehemently. The task with which they had been commissioned weighed heavily upon them: the inescapable obligation to bear witness. They are no longer to make their own choices. God himself had placed his hand upon them. They must speak of that which they " had seen and heard." They were fully aware of the authority and the rights of the Sanhedrin. As Jewish observers of the law, they respected its injunctions. We gain an inkling of this from the words of refusal which they had used; they explained to the Supreme Council that the decision to act or not to act was indeed the subject matter of the judgment, but also a judgment that they had to decide according to their conscience.

They had, however, already made up their minds. The *Holy Spirit* had enlightened and strengthened them while they were arriving at their decision. According to Plato, Socrates had replied to his judges, " I honor and love you, but I would rather obey God than you "; and Sophocles, the poet, in the tragedy of Antigones put this into the mouth of his hero: " I do not wish to fall into the hands of the vengeful gods simply because I showed fear in the presence of arrogant men." What differentiates the words of the apostle from such praiseworthy testimony on behalf of the rights of conscience is that in them the supreme personal experience of salvation in Christ Jesus is made manifest.

The Strengthening of the Prayerful Community (4:23-31)

[23]After they had been released, they returned to their companions and reported to them all that the high priests and elders of the people had said to them. [24]When the faithful heard these things, they raised their voices to God with one accord and said, " Lord, you are he who ' created heaven and earth and the sea that is in them ' (Ex. 20:11). [25]You have spoken by the voice of your servant, David, our father, through the Holy Spirit, ' Why did the Gentiles rage and the people plot inanities? [26]The kings of the earth rose up in array and the possessors of power connive against the Lord and his Anointed One ' (Ps. 21:1f.). [27]True enough, in this city there were gathered together against your holy servant, Jesus, whom you have anointed, both Herod and Pontius Pilate with the Gentiles and the peoples of Israel [28]to wreak upon him whatever your hand and your plan had predestined to take place. [29]And now, Lord, consider their threats and give to your servants courage to preach your word, [30]while

you exercise your power to heal and to work wonders and signs through the use of your holy servant, Jesus."

This passage is closely related to the narrative of the healing of the man born lame. At the same time it gives us a profound insight into the thinking and the faith of the community. It is a highly suggestive contrast to the preceding scene, in which the Sanhedrin had played the leading role. If we are conscious of the jealousy, of the uncertainty and helplessness of the authorities confronted by the people, so we are aware of the *sincerity, of the certainty and unanimity* of the Christian community. This community, as we observe again, is bound to the Jewish community by intimate ties; it still offers its prayers in traditional concepts and after the norms of Old Testament texts, but over and over again the novelty and the uniqueness of the Christian salvation experience finds an outlet in its own separate thoughts and motives. It is again a text of the psalms from which the church reads her history and by which she expresses the certitude of her faith. This is again a very graphic, a very realistic example of how Old Testament passages are viewed and interpreted in the light of the New Testament experience of salvation.

Here again, in this prayer, there is revealed the especial concern of the primitive church to proclaim the " good news," when the author explicitly stresses the inability of the opposition to interfere with the plans of God. In fact, by their actions against Jesus, the persecutors of the church eventually and unwittingly *realize the salvific will of God.* This thought, which we encounter repeatedly in the Acts of the Apostles, not only seeks to answer the scandal of the passion, but also gives us an insight into the courage of the community confronting the jealousy of

the Jewish authorities. God, who permitted the plotting of the
enemies against Jesus, in fact fitted it into the fulfillment of his
plan of salvation; he who possessed the power to shield his
messengers—who are here called the servants of God, not
without reason—is also able to guide them to the successful
accomplishment of their mission, that is, to bear witness in spite
of opposition.

[31]*When they had prayed, the place where they gathered rocked
with an earthquake, and all were filled with the Holy Spirit,
and they boldly proclaimed the word of God.*

Three times the word " boldly " is used in the passages which
we are considering (4 : 13, 29, 31). As a happy tune it pervades
the narrative and resounds emphatically and clearly. The reason
is obvious: to enable us to recognize unmistakably the fundamental attitude of the primitive church towards the persecution
by the Sanhedrin. The word " boldly " enunciates the cheerful
consciousness of the infant church, which has its source in the
living experience of salvific grace, in the assured knowledge
of the proximity of the Lord who asserts his presence by the
testimony of the Holy Spirit. It is important for the nascent
church to proclaim in a graphic manner the mystery of the Spirit
as a continuing and continuously effective Pentecost because of
the dangers which threaten her, for in this way she is fortified
anew in " the courage " which she manifests. When we read
that " all were filled with the Holy Spirit," we must remember
that this " fulfillment " had now manifested itself outwardly.
Furthermore, we should obviously also think of that mysterious
preaching, of which we have an inkling in the sermon on
Pentecost, which is expressly attested to as a sign of the Holy
Spirit (10 : 44ff.; 19 : 6).

Does not such information sound like something remote and strange, a fable of sorts? Is all this actually worthy of credence? And does it frankly belong to the image of the church? Or has the church already become antiquated and static, since according to our own perceptiveness we can detect so little in her which made her so attractive and a community enjoying youthful vigor? Should not those extraordinary gifts of the Holy Spirit which we call charismata have been important from the very outset, as she was about to set out on her journey through the world with the purpose of gaining it for Christ? Could not the church of today regain her pristine courage and her original effectiveness were she to preserve a constant contact with *the living experience of the Spirit?*

The New Image of the Community (4:32—5:16)

"ONE HEART AND ONE MIND" (4:32-37)

A new " collection of narratives "—as exegetes are accustomed to call it—is here interpolated. Verses 2:42-47 had already detailed a similar set of stories. As far as content is concerned the two passages are interwoven and form a trinity, if we consider them together with 5:12-16. From this trinity fundamentally the same image emerges, although perhaps occasionally one or the other is more emphatically stressed. It is as if the author intended again to afford us and thus to ready us for that reverential gaze at the activity of the Holy Spirit at work in the community of the Lord.

[32] *All the faithful were aware of one heart and one mind, and not a single one among them called anything he possessed his own, but everything was held in common.* [33] *With ever greater power*

*the apostles bore witness to the resurrection of the Lord Jesus and
all were filled with great grace. ³⁴There was not one among them
to be found in need. All those who owned farms or houses sold
them, brought the proceeds of the sales, ³⁵placed them at the feet
of the apostles; and it was divided among them each according to
his need.*

Much more vividly than in the first narrative, the *heroic services
of the brotherhood* among the faithful are here projected into the
foreground. The phrase which today has become axiomatic:
" one heart and one mind," literally derived its origin from this
biblical passage, as do so many other phrases and figures of
speech in the language of our everyday life. This harmony of
heart and mind found its most perfect manifestation in the selfless
renunciation of all personal property, when the needs of others
demanded it. As we have already said previously (2:44f.), it was
a spontaneous outburst of fraternal charity, prompted by the
experience of salvation and the example of Christ, and in no way
compulsory either by law or by force. Everyone was at liberty to
do with his property as he wished, as we learn a few lines later
on and then with crushing force in the words of Peter to
Ananias (5:4). Hence it is deliberate intent that it is restated
for us here: " Not a single one among them called anything he
possessed his own, but everything was held in common." The
right to and the privilege of owning private property was not in-
fringed upon; but more compelling than any right or any law
was the readiness, the willingness to renounce it that others
might enjoy it. And this renunciation derived from being
smitten by the supreme value of faith and of hope in the Lord.

³⁶*Joseph, who had received the surname of Barnabas (which
means of encouragement) from the other apostles, a Levite, who*

stemmed from Cyprus, sold a piece of land, ³⁷which he owned,
brought the proceeds and placed it at the feet of the apostles.

These sentences serve as an additional stroke to the total picture
of the church which has thus far been etched. It presents us with
an example of the service of the brotherhood which has already
been sketched and offers at the same time a hint that the statement that " all " had sold their lands or their dwellings may be
considered as a popular hyperbolic generalization. If all had
actually sold all they had, there would be no reason to stress the
action of Joseph Barnabas as something especially worthy of note.
Likewise the words of Peter would appear to be little worthy of
credence (in 5:4); the same is true of later passages in the Acts
of the Apostles where the possession of private property is taken
for granted, as for example when the house of Mary, the mother
of Mark, is mentioned (12:12).

When Joseph Barnabas is singled out for such special treatment, there may have been a special reason, perhaps the fact that
he had later on a role, a special task to perform in the future upbuilding of the church. As we learn from verses 11:22ff. Barnabas
was commissioned by the mother community at Jerusalem to
take care of and to rule over the first gentile community grouped
together in Antioch, since he was " an excellent man, filled with
the Holy Spirit and abounding in faith." It was he who summoned Saul of Tarsus for this missionary task and from then on
determined his further course of action.

The Condemnation of Ananias and Saphira (5:1–11)

¹*A man by the name of Ananias together with his wife Saphira*
sold an estate (piece of property), but with the knowledge of his

wife ²he kept back some of the proceeds for himself and taking only a part of it laid it at the feet of the apostles.

In these two short verses we are introduced to a story which not only casts a dark shadow over the community which hitherto had been depicted in glorious colors, but also fills us even today with consternation—which even frightens us because of the terrible punishment which is meted out to the culprits. In accordance with the intention of the author, the narrative forms a sad and sorrowful conclusion to the two previous pictures which he had drawn. Verses 4:32–35 delineate in glowing terms the broad image of the heroic services of the brotherhood in the renunciation and self-sacrifice of personal property and adds to it in 4:36f. the spectacularly praiseworthy and heroic example of Joseph Barnabas. Now the Acts of the Apostles feels compelled to report a sinful deed which took place within the inner circle of the infant church. The fact that Luke does not attempt to pass over this incident in silence strengthens our confidence both in his conscientiousness and in his credibility.

³Peter said, "Ananias, why has Satan filled your heart, so that you defraud the Holy Spirit and keep back for yourself a part of the proceeds you have received from your estate? ⁴Would it not have remained yours, if you had not sold it? And even after its sale would not the proceeds have been at your disposal? What got into you to do such a thing? You have not lied to your fellow men, but to God!" ⁵When Ananias heard these words, he fell to the ground and died, and a great fear came upon all who heard it. ⁶The young men, however, rose, wrapped him up, carried him out and buried him.

Again Peter dominates the scene. He is pictured to us here as possessing absolute power in the office which he held. Up to the present we have looked upon him more as the responsible spokesman and nuntius of the community. In the cure of the man born lame he revealed himself as the wielder of the power of healing, which had been conferred upon him *ex officio*. From now on he will step forward as the possessor of supernatural knowledge and of judicial power, which enable him to decide between life and death for transgressions. Could the magnitude and the power of the apostolic office be described more vividly than this?

We are made to feel how concerned our narrator is about making clear how close the presence of Jesus Christ in the Holy Spirit actually is and how he seeks to present the church in all her holiness and innocence. Why the church should be concerned about this is made clear by the exclamation of Peter: " *You have not lied to your fellow men but to God!"* Can we today, who are so inclined to look upon the church as just another phenomenon of everyday life, at least insofar as her sensible reality is concerned, interiorly grasp and without hesitation affirm the truth which is expressed in this passage from Peter?

With what justification can the apostle say that Ananias has lied to God? The first sentence gives us the reason: "Ananias, why has Satan filled your heart, so that you defraud the Holy Spirit and keep back for yourself a part of the proceeds which you have received for your estate?" In what does the sin against God consist? In the embezzled and secreted sum of money? It could not have been a large sum! It was not the money itself. Ananias was not obligated in any way to hand it over, just as he was in no way bound to sell his land. This is stated unmistakably in the very next sentence. We already know that community sharing of property was purely voluntary on the part of the faithful.

Where is the guilt therefore to be found? We know what it was and because of our knowledge we ought to be deeply horrified. It was *the lie* by which he pretended to give to Peter the entire proceeds of the sale. What made the lie so heinous? We would rather pose the question this way because we are so shaken by it. Indeed, it must have been much more grievous than we would perhaps care to think about seriously. What is Peter? What is the community before which Ananias is arraigned? It is the *work of Jesus Christ*, the work of the Holy Spirit.

[7]*After an interval of about three hours, it came to pass that his wife came in, not knowing what had taken place.* [8]*Peter said to her, " Tell me. Did you sell the piece of land for so much?" And she said, " Yes, for so and so much." * [9]*Peter, however, replied to her, " Why have both of you conspired together to tempt the Spirit of the Lord? Listen to the feet of the men who have been burying your husband and will also carry you out." * [10]*She fell at his feet on the spot and died. The young men entered, found her dead and carried her out and buried her alongside her husband.*

We are not going to spend any time discussing the literary artistry with which Luke portrays both these events and synchronizes them so carefully with what went before; here we are more interested in the religious pronouncements and in the salvation-theological considerations which pervade the narrative. The appearance of Ananias's wife on the scene furnishes Peter with the opportunity to make visible the complete reprobation of the plot of the wicked couple. The wife knew about *the plan of concealment and also the falsehood* it entailed. They had

mutually agreed upon the lie; this much is clear from the fact
that she knew the exact amount of money her husband had
turned over to Peter. Who was the instigator of the plot and the
more responsible of the two? Nothing is said on this score. In
some way we are reminded of another couple, that couple which
in the very beginning went astray because of their non-observance
of a command of God, and how both of them suffered the
punishment God meted out.

One of the phrases of the narrative sounds a bit odd: " She
fell at his feet on the spot and died." Why odd? Because the
phrase " at his feet " is repeated several times in the narrative.
The individual stages of the plot are arranged in climactic order,
and end in the meaningful statement concerning the *position
and the plenary powers* of the apostles. In 4:32 we are told that
the members of the community sold their lands and their homes
and placed the proceeds of what was disposed of " at the feet of
the apostles." Of Joseph Barnabas it is reported that he also
placed the money that he had received from the sale of his
property " at the feet of the apostles " (4:37). And in the same
figurative language it is also remarked of Ananias that he too
" placed at the feet of the apostles " only that part of the proceeds which he wished to hand over. By this figurative language,
by which the powerful position and authority of the apostles
within the community were depicted so graphically for us, all
three segments of the story are skillfully drawn together in
accordance with literary dictates uppermost in the mind of the
author. Thus it is hardly happenstance when it is said of Saphira
that she fell dead at the feet of the apostle Peter. For Saphira
had sinned against the plenitude of power which had been
handed over to Peter by Christ himself, the true head of the
community.

[11]A great fear seized upon the whole community and upon all those who heard it.

This sentence not only concludes the narrative, but also discloses the special significance to be attached to the condemnation of the guilty pair. Of course, the punishment meted out to Ananias and Saphira was intended for them personally—no matter how much we would like to conjecture on their ultimate fate in the sight of God. By their death everything pernicious in their action was removed from the hallowed precincts of the community. At the same time it was intended that all men, the members of the community as well as those without the fold, should be taught how relentlessly adamant the Lord watches over the purity and the guiltlessness of his " holy ones " (9:13). The " fear " which enveloped all was intended, as a consequence, to serve as a means of protecting and preserving the inviolability of the church and of inculcating *a wholesome and salvific reverence for the mysteries of the Holy Spirit* which had been confided to her. It is the same Spirit which guides and strengthens the church against all persecutions from without and empowers her to confront crises which might arise within—all the result of the frailty of mankind.

THE GROWING ESTEEM OF THE APOSTLES (5:12–16)

[12]Many signs and wonders were worked among the people through the hands of the apostles. They were all gathered together in the portico of Solomon; [13]none of the others, however, dared join them, but the people spoke highly of them.

[14]Larger and larger grew the number of those who believed in the Lord, groups of both men and women. [15]So it became a custom that many in fact carried the sick into the narrow streets and placed them on beds and pallets, so that when Peter passed by, at least his shadow might fall upon some of them. [16]Throngs from the surrounding cities also flocked toward Jerusalem, bringing the sick and those pestered with unclean spirits, and they were all cured.

At the time that the man born lame was healed, we were given to understand what the gift of healing meant to the apostles in their role as witnesses. This charism was given not only as a service of beneficent love for the sick, but also as a proof that the curative powers which Jesus had manifested while passing through the countryside were still present in his church. In its profoundest sense we witness in the healing power of the apostles the *life-mystery in the resurrection of Jesus* and the *power of faith* in an exalted and ever-present Lord. We could not do justice to the mystery here were we to attempt to explain it simply in terms of the purely natural.

It may be that those persons who placed their sick in the streets consciously placed their confidence in the healing power of the shadow of Peter. If they did so with this in mind, they were motivated by various erroneous and naïve considerations. This does not, however, detract from the factual reason for which the cures took place. Let us recall how in the case of the crippled man Peter had to resort to a speech in order to dissuade the crowd from indulging in their superstitions. But this was not enough. He then attempted to guide them to Jesus whose name effected the cure in union, of course, with their faith in him.

Again before the Sanhedrin (5:17-42)

THE ARREST AND THE RELEASE OF THE APOSTLES (5:17-24)

[17]*Then the high priest and all his followers, namely, the parties of the Sadducees, rose up to a man, and animated by jealousy* [18]*they laid their hands on the apostles and put them into a public prison.* [19]*At night, however, an angel of the Lord threw open the doors of the prison, led them outside and admonished them,* [20]*" Go, put in an appearance in the temple and proclaim to the people all the words of this life!"* [21a]*And after they heard this, at daybreak the next day they entered into the temple and taught.*

This repeated disobedience against the authorities of the temple does not need to be stressed unduly in order to show its connection with the preceding story. As soon as they had been released with a sharp and definite admonition to abstain from using the name of Jesus (4:17ff.) after their hearing by the Sanhedrin, the apostles felt themselves obligated to God rather than to men. This does not imply that they did not acknowledge, both dutifully and respectfully, the jurisdiction of the Jewish authorities (4:19). In the task entrusted to them by the Risen One, they recognized that they were commissioned to give testimony and they remembered that this obligation had been imposed upon them by God himself. *Their own consciences* bound them to speak of what they as authenticated witnesses of God's revelation had learned. " It is impossible for us to keep silent about what we have seen and heard " (4:21a), they had retorted as they were released by the Sanhedrin.

Now the apostles are again in prison. It may have been the same cell into which they had been thrown when they were arrested the first time, even though this time the bailiwick is designated as " the public prison." On this occasion, however, it would appear as if all the twelve were affected by the measures which the authorities employed. The task of bearing witness which had been laid upon them by the Risen One is here shown to be the dominant consideration in all their lives; on this occasion they give tangible evidence of their concern. On the next day the trial, their trial, is to begin. What is in store for them? They must be ready for anything and everything. They must stand in judgment before the same court before which Jesus himself had stood and received his death sentence.

The Risen One, however, grants them a sign. And this sign was intended not only for them but also for their enemies in the Sanhedrin. *God testifies to his presence.* " An angel of the Lord " led them out of prison. This took place in a way which we cannot now explain. It could be looked upon as some kind of huge joke, if the motives at play were not so grimly in earnest. The angel gives them a task : they were to do precisely the very same thing for which they had been jailed. They were to go before the people and to proclaim to them " the words of this life."

21b*The high priest, however, and his followers came together, summoned the Sanhedrin and the entire senate of the sons of Israel and sent to the prison to have the prisoners brought before them.* 22*When the servants arrived there and failed to find them in the prison, they returned and made their report;* 23*" We found the prison securely bolted and the sentries posted at the gates, but when we opened the portals, we found no one inside."* 24*Now, when they heard these words, the captain of the temple and the* *high priests were thrown into greater consternation and asked one another, what all this would come to.*

The Acts of the Apostles takes great delight in depicting over and over again the helplessness, the perplexity, and the embarrassment of the foes of the early church. The picture which the passage paints does not dispense with the comical, either. Aware of what the apostles were doing, the high priests, that is, those outstanding personages who connived in the arrest, the Sadduceean party of priests, nonetheless were present at this special session of the Sanhedrin and, seated, awaited the appearance of the prisoners. The temple police searched thoroughly and fruitlessly the cells of the prisoners which were untampered with outwardly. At that very moment the supposed prisoners were in the temple enclosure and proclaimed to an attentive audience their message of the " good news " of resurrection and life. The consciousness of the power which these officials possessed was replaced by sentiments of distress. Would it not have occurred to them that *a power mightier than their own* was taking a part in the proceedings? Of course, our text betrays nothing of this. Might not the more earnest thinkers among them have taken the affair more seriously and considered it as a warning being offered them? Was not Gamaliel one of those who might have weighed in the balance the possible intervention of God? His words, which we shall soon hear, would appear to substantiate such a theory.

THE RELEASE OF THE APOSTLES AND THE PROGRESS OF THE CHURCH (5:25-42)

[25]*Then one of their number came and reported to them, " Look, the men whom you threw into prison are in the temple and are*

teaching the people." ²⁶*Thereupon, the captain and his officers went there and led them back, without employing forceful measures; for they were afraid that they might be stoned by the people.* ²⁷*They brought them and stood them before the Supreme Council, and the high priest questioned them and said,* ²⁸*" Did we not expressly forbid you to preach in this name? And now you have filled all Jerusalem with your teaching and you are determined to fix the responsibility for this man's blood upon us."*

Ever more clearly the Jewish leaders must have felt their power-lessness in comparison to the *life-power of the community of Jesus.* This is brought to our attention with unexpected graphic-ness in this present questioning. As in its first juridical encounter with Peter and John, when the undeniable presence of the man born lame made it impossible for the Supreme Council to deal with them as they had first intended, so now it is the empty cell which demonstrates to the councillors how difficult it is to assail the life-power of a movement set in motion by the Holy Spirit.

What an unbearable challenge it must have been to their consciousness of power, when the councillors were apprised of the fact that the very persons whom they had taken into custody were, of all places, in the temple and, of all things, preaching the doctrine for which the authorities were trying to build up a case against them. Worst of all, in their eyes at least, was the fact that the people had gathered so enthusiastically around them and listened so attentively to their words. How tenuous the power of the Sanhedrin and its police had become ever since they had aligned against the church—this helplessness the captain of the temple along with his officers experienced when they were com-

pelled to conduct the apostles back to the assembly of the Sanhedrin without employing either force or blows because they
were surrounded by crowds of people who were prepared to stone
them even though they were the official agents of the supreme
governing body of the Jews.

Was the Sanhedrin agitated by something else besides fear of
the people? The words of the high priest suggest something extremely curious. Do they not show signs of fear and anxiety?
First of all, they contain an accusation. It could not be anything
else. The high priest reminds the apostles of the express prohibition that they had received " not to teach in this name " (4:17f.).
Again he refrains from mentioning the name upon which everything is focussed. Is this out of contempt for Jesus? Is it a kind
of shyness? We might possibly lean towards this last hypothesis.
For there is a curious kind of concern expressed in his words,
when he remarks about the *blood of this man*. The blood of
Jesus is what he actually wants to say. That blood which on a
previous occasion the misguided people had called down upon
themselves, when Jesus was condemned by Pilate: " His blood
be upon us and upon our children " (Mt. 27:25). In his gospel,
Luke does not reproduce this phrase, but he knew of it and
makes up for its lack by referring to it here, when he puts it into
the mouth of the high priest.

*29Peter and the apostles replied, " We must obey God rather than
man. 30The God of our fathers raised Jesus from the dead, him
whom you have hung upon a tree and killed. 31God raised him
up to his right hand as prince and saviour, that he might bring
Israel to repentance and the forgiveness of sins. 32We are, however, witnesses to these deeds, and witness also is the Holy Spirit
whom God has bestowed upon those who obey him." 33When*

they heard this, they were enraged and plotted together how they might kill them.

The answer of the apostles to the charges alleged against them by the Sanhedrin is not couched in that language which might be expected of accused persons. It is directed, rather, against the accusers, and this by means of a *courageous profession of faith.* There is a very palpable difference between this reply and their attitude at the first hearing where, though there was no cowardly toadying on the part of the apostles, there was nevertheless a certain reserve, a certain caution shown towards the supreme tribunal of the Jews. This time they no longer submit to the judgment of the Sanhedrin. Now, clearly and without any reservation the words which fall from their lips resound throughout the courtroom: " We must obey God rather than men."

Now the hour had arrived when it became evident that a new order, a new institution was being established, one which must inevitably clash with the supreme Jewish authorities. It was the message of Jesus, the " good news " which he proclaimed and the testimony which was to be offered for him, which ever since the Pentecost event compelled men to make a *fateful decision, a choice of belief.* The Sanhedrin steeled its heart to the challenge of the hour. The mystery of salvation which was presented by God to men in Jesus of Nazareth had already in the trial of Jesus been dismissed by the court of last instance. And now again, since the apostles of this same Jesus sought anew to preach by their " good news " the way of salvation announced by Christ Jesus, they had to confront the Jewish leaders. This is a truly tragic situation; it could cause only disaster. This will inevitably happen wherever the living summons of God and the testimony of the Holy Spirit encounter the power structure of inflexible tradition and static institutions, neither of which is willing or capable of heeding the summons directed to them. This was the situation in which the Sanhedrin found itself when Jesus stood before it and was condemned to death. Now this court is again faced with the same situation, since it again demands unconditional obedience, this time from the apostles.

The apostles must have deeply felt the schism into which they had been thrust or were causing. They had, however, made up their minds. *The task with which the Risen One had entrusted them* weighed heavily upon them. It was the task of him who has shown himself to be alive and had revealed himself in the God-mystery, the task of him who had on Pentecost sent the Holy Spirit and since then had manifested his power in signs and miracles. It was impossible for them to do anything less than what they were doing. This Peter himself under oath had declared at his trial: he could not remain silent concerning what they had seen and heard.

They stood before the Supreme Council of the Jews. They *had to give an answer.* They did so fully aware of the task for which they had been commissioned. Their reply, as it is found in the narrative of the Acts of the Apostles, is expressed in a few pithy words, each of which is, however, filled with meaning; each contains an essential statement. Their answer is a profession of faith, a profession of faith and a witness, an appeal, and a promise. It is an appeal meant to awaken a response; an appeal which the infant church directs to the synagogue, which shows itself to be adamant.

Again, the message of Christ rings throughout the hall as their first and most powerful witness, that message which up to the present we have always considered to be the first and most decisive profession made by the apostles: *The God of our*

Fathers has raised Jesus from the dead. The formulation of this statement is carefully worded. " The God of our fathers " are the words which the apostle chose in full awareness of their import. He does not wish to address them as a stranger, as one who is beyond the pale of Judaism. No, his God is also the God of the members of this very Sanhedrin and is therefore the God of their fathers, the God of Israel, the God of Abraham, Isaac, and Jacob, as Peter had also addressed Him shortly before in his speech on behalf of the healing of the man born lame (3:13). With this reference to the " God of our fathers " Peter likewise appeals to the entire history of revelation as credible testimony for his message.

On this momentous occasion, Peter specifies Jesus of Nazareth as *prince and saviour,* sitting at the right hand of God. By so doing he attributes to him the supreme honors which in the language of the Old Testament are ascribed only to God. This prince and saviour has been raised up to bring that salvation to Israel for which the prophets had so long awaited, that salvation which includes repentance and the forgiveness of sins. We may see in the words of Peter a profoundly meaningful allusion which we will meet again in Paul, namely, ". . . whom you have hung upon a tree and have killed " (see also 10:39), which he may have meant to refer to a passage in the Book of Deuteronomy : "And if any man is punished by death for a crime which demands the death sentence and you hang him on a tree, his corpse should not remain overnight hanging on a tree, but you should bury him on the same day, for a hanged man is accursed by God " (Deut. 21:22ff.).

In these concise words the answer of Peter circumlocutes the economy of salvation which has been planned by God. The name of God is repeated three times in the passage : " The God of our fathers raised Jesus from the dead. . . , God has bestowed the Holy Spirit upon those who obey him. . . , God has raised him up to his right hand as prince and saviour. . . ." And on this awareness is based the introductory profession of faith: "We must obey God rather than man." *Justification and an appeal* are embodied in these words of the apostle: justification for the message which they preach in the name of Christ; an appeal to the men of the Sanhedrin to whose insight and openness is coupled the salvation of the people.

How did the Council members receive this appeal? They persisted in their delusion; and their resistance was even stronger than before. *"When they heard this, they were enraged and plotted together how they might kill them."* They decline to accept the insight which is proferred them. Here again there is repeated what Jesus himself must have experienced. They examine ways and means of liquidating the troublesome witnesses and admonishers. They act as guardians of an order which they regarded as divine, although the divinely revealed witness of this order—as the Acts of the Apostles has already exhibited him to us thus far—has borne testimony to the veracity of the salvation event in Christ Jesus, and so thereby the right of the apostles to announce the " good news " which he had brought

[34]*But a Pharisee in the Sanhedrin, by the name of Gamaliel, a teacher of the law, held in esteem by all the people, stood up; he moved that they be removed for a short while* [35]*and then he spoke to his confreres, " You men of Israel, weigh well what you intend to do to these men.* [36]*Before our time Theodas revolted and he maintained that he was someone extraordinary. A group of men to the number of some four hundred allied themselves to him; he was killed, all who had joined him were scattered and*

came to nought. ³⁷ *After him, there arose Judas the Galilean, in the days of the census and he attracted people to his cause. He also perished and all who had joined him were dispersed."*

The Risen One watches over his witnesses. Their work is not yet finished. In the language of John's gospel we could say, " Their hour had not yet come " (Jn. 7 : 3; 18 : 20). The Holy Spirit pilots the bark of the infant church in these critical hours. This is demonstrated satisfactorily by the intervention of Gamaliel, the Pharisee. He was a highly regarded theologian and teacher of the law. This is also corroborated for us by the writings of rabbinical Judaism, preserved for us in the Talmud. This man enjoys a special place in the Acts of the Apostles because of the fact that in a very dark hour, Paul the apostle appeals to him in the presence of an enraged Jewish populace, when Paul asserts that he " was instructed at the feet of Gamaliel in accordance with the severity of the law of your fathers as a Zealot for God " (22 : 3).

Gamaliel is introduced to us as a Pharisee. This is done deliberately. For in reading the Acts of the Apostles we receive the impression that the Pharisees did not appear to be either as hostile or as fanatical towards the apostles as were the Sadducees and the officials of the temple. On this score we should read the account of the trial of Paul before the Sanhedrin, where, confronted by the hatred of the priestly party, Paul was able nevertheless to gain the sympathy of the Pharisees and to arouse dissension among the supreme authorities of the Jews which redounded to his favor. Luke frequently suggests that the hostility of certain parties among the Jewish people should not be ascribed to the Jewish people as a whole.

What thoughts and what designs moved Gamaliel to act as he

did? He knew about the party of the Sadducees who were guided in their deliberations by power politics. He had experienced first-hand their tactics in the trial of Jesus. For we should take for granted that he was present at these fateful sessions. Such men as Nicodemus (Jn. 3:1; 7:50) and Joseph of Arimathea (Lk. 23:50) also belonged to the Sanhedrin. Gamaliel was also aware of the *injustice that had been done Jesus*. He hoped by a delaying action to prevent another injustice.

Gamaliel singles out two examples. The movement which Judas the Galilean initiated was still evident at the time of Jesus and even later in the continued existence of a party called the Zealots. But these attempts at rebellion failed to succeed and in fact incited the occupying forces to greater watchfulness and prompted them to make severe reprisals. In the gospel of Luke we find an example of such an insurrection, when we are told of the Galilean " whose blood Pilate mingled with the sacrifices " (Lk. 13:1ff.).

[38]*"And in this present case I say to you, stay away from these men and leave them alone; for should this plan and this work be of men, it will be brought to nought.* [39a]*If it is of God, you cannot destroy it. It could even be that you might find yourselves fighting against God!"*

A profound reason behind Gamaliel's intervention is indicated by these words. He knows that God is the *Lord of human history*. The fate of the Jewish people, as this is manifested in sacred scriptures, enforces his judgment. The events of the recent past made only more profound his knowledge and experience of the ways of God. What did he think of Jesus of Nazareth? His words of themselves reveal nothing on this score. He knew of

Jesus' death. We cannot doubt this. Did he know anything more? Should he not have known of other extraordinary events which had taken place since his death? Of the miracles and signs of the apostles? Of the community? Surely he must have been struck by the appearance of the accused and by the force of his testimony.

Gamaliel is animated not only by sheer prudence and by calculated expediency, but also by his knowledge of God, who—this is his reasoning—could have taken an active part in the work of the apostles. Although we may not be able to penetrate into the ultimate considerations which moved this man to act as he did, we may however be thankful for his tact and prudence by which course the church was protected from a danger which —humanly speaking—was much greater than it now appears to us. Again we are apprised of the fact that *a superior power* holds sway over the church: the power and the love of the Holy Spirit.

³⁹ᵇ*They agreed with him,* ⁴⁰*summoned the apostles back, had them flogged, and warned them not to speak in the name of Jesus, and set them free.* ⁴¹*These however left the presence of the Sanhedrin overjoyed that they had been found worthy to suffer humiliation for his name.*

And what must we think: after this dangerous and threatening trial had been concluded in such a happy fashion, *the apostles were flogged*. The Sanhedrin ordered this punishment to be inflicted and by so doing tried to save face as the supreme authority in Judaism. The flogging was designed as a chastisement for the non-observance of its prohibition not to teach. Paul also had to undergo this punishment five times (2 Cor. 11:24), which as a rule consisted of thirty-nine lashes (forty save one), since the

Jews were reluctant about exceeding the number forty. In his eschatological sermon Jesus said, " They will deliver you up to the tribunals; you will be scourged in the synagogues and you will be arraigned before princes and kings for my sake, to give testimony to them " (Mk. 13:9). We need not be reminded of the scourging of Jesus in the story of the passion. Pilate said to the Jews, " I will therefore discipline him and then set him free " (Lk. 23:16). And in John's gospel we are told that the Roman procurator sought to save Jesus from death by having him scourged—but in vain.

In a happy, if not joyous, state of mind the apostles left the Sanhedrin. It was the joyfulness of men who were so pervaded by their belief in Christ Jesus that they were more than happy to share with their Lord and Master both *humiliation and disgrace.* Their gaze was raised above and beyond their own private debasement and directed to him of whose *majesty* they were cognizant. Belief in the resurrection and in the exaltation of Christ rendered all things to little value in contrast to the hope which so indestructibly filled their hearts. Paul gives us an inkling of a soul permeated by this hope when he writes in his letter to the Romans, " We exult also in the possession of our hope in sharing in the glory of God. But we exult not only in this, but also in our tribulations, since we are aware that tribulation generates patience, patience endurance, and endurance hope " (Rom. 5:22ff.).

[42]*Nor did they desist from teaching daily in the temple and from house to house, nor from preaching the good news of Jesus Christ.*

With this sentence the author concludes the first series of narratives of the Acts of the Apostles. This series was centered upon the *mother community* in Jerusalem, upon its beginnings and supernatural searchings, its blossoming and growth within the framework of Judaism, and upon its struggles and its triumphs over threats from within and from without.

THE INTERNAL AND EXTERNAL
DEVELOPMENT OF THE CHURCH:
FROM JERUSALEM TO ANTIOCH
(6:1—12:25)

A new epoch now unfolds. The number of the faithful increases. The responsibilities and the anxieties of the apostles, the twelve, also multiply. The apostles encounter dangers. Tensions, humanly understandable in such a community, crop up repeatedly. The apostles are on the lookout for helpers and collaborators who are willing to serve the community. A memorable and significant development is inaugurated. The church advances bravely into newer time-space dimensions of history. In her task, in her dedication to " all people " and " for all peoples " (Mt. 28:17), and in her commitment to bear witness " to the ends of the world " (1:8), we see that she must unfold her mission and the fullness of her power and must share with others the office which comes from Christ. An organism, such as the church projects, bears within itself the germ of growth which will remain vital throughout the centuries. Repeatedly the law of continuing renewal will manifest itself, as long as the church exists among men and seeks to serve mankind.

Seven men are added to the twelve. They are men who are officially appointed. We are made acquainted with their zeal and with their willingness to spread the message of salvation, the " good news." They fulfill their duties with a holy fervor. They will compel men to make a substantive choice. They arouse opposition and suffer from persecution. This will be the first persecution of the Christian church. The church suffers the first martyrdom in the full sense of the word, and this disperses the greater part of the community over the countryside. But the dispersed, those of the diaspora, become witnesses and advocates throughout the country. This thought brings

into harmony various passages and individual incidents in chapters
6–12, even though they are derived from various sources. Beginning
in Jerusalem, the first center of Judeo-Christian Christianity, the
message travels through the Palestinian country of the Jews and
brings about the establishment of a new center of missionary activity
in Antioch of Syria by the founding of the first gentile Christian
community there.

The "Seven" (6:1—8:40)

The Selection and the Appointment (6:1–7)

*¹In those days as the number of the apostles increased, the Greeks
began to murmur against the Hebrews because their widows
were neglected in the daily distribution of alms. ²The twelve
then called together the entire body of the disciples and said,
" It is not our duty that we give up the word of God and devote
ourselves to waiting upon tables. ³Therefore, brethren, look
around for seven men who enjoy a good reputation, full of the
Spirit and of wisdom; these we shall appoint for this service.
⁴We wish, rather, to devote ourselves wholly and entirely to
prayer and to the ministry of the Word."*

In the phrase " in those days " and in the designation of the
faithful as " disciples "—literally pupils, a form of address
which had hitherto never been used—we are given to understand
that a new segment in the structure is beginning to be laid.
Moreover, *the image of the community* becomes more animated
and richer than ever before. The church is, however, still living
in close contact with non-Christian Judaism. In the narrative,
which unfolds, we are informed that the community comes

together of its own accord and also takes care of the needy. For the difficulty that is raised and one which is the subject of the narrative arises within the community itself. The occasion for it is supplied by the charity which is practiced towards the needy. For we must interpret the phrase " the daily distribution of alms " in 6:1 and the reference to the " widows " precisely in this sense.

Even in Jesus' own lifetime, *charity* was a part of the work which the disciples performed. This virtue is of the very essence of the mission of the church. For in its practice the basic commandment of fraternal charity receives its tangible, visual expression. The fulfillment of this charitable task will by its very nature always encounter, and sometimes be rendered nugatory by, the self-interest and jealousy of men. Where is the man or the institution which has not at one time or the other experienced the sad fact that even with the maximum expenditure of effort he can scarcely do justice to all the requests which are made of him, to all the expectations which are centered upon him? The poor are easily hurt and show themselves as demanding in their poverty and as fastidious in their traits of character as anyone else. This is especially so when there are rivalries and jealousies among the various groups of people dependent on charity.

This appears to have been the case in the community at Jerusalem. There we come to know *Hellenists* and *Hebrews*. Both are Israelites. They differ, however, both in language and mode of life. Hellenists are those Jews who were reared in the environment of Greek culture. This might mean that some of them stem from the Jewish diaspora which extended over the entire Mediterranean basin and that others lived in territories in and around Palestine in which the Greek tongue and the Greek way of life predominated ever since the emergence of Hellenistic culture under the aegis of Alexander the Great. Such a Hellenist was Barnabas, who according to Acts 4:36 traced his origin to Cyprus; and also Saul, who came from Tarsus in Cilicia, although membership in a distinct group did not appear to be governed only by the language spoken or by the place of origin.

The apostles were aware of the difficulty. They were also conscious of their own limitations. It appears that up to this point they had personally supervised the ministry of charity in the care of the poor. Now they begin to experience more desperately the pressure which was being exerted upon them when they tried to perform the personal and exclusive task which was theirs in addition to meeting the demands made upon them by duties of charity. Their own special and essential task is clearly paraphrased in this passage. "It is not our duty that we give up the word of God," they declare in the beginning. And then they immediately give a description, and not as an afterthought, of what is essential to their ministry: "We wish, rather, to devote ourselves wholly and entirely to prayer and to the ministry of the word." By saying this, they did not downgrade the charitable work that was being done. Rather, they knew full well the hierarchy of duties and the primary purpose of the task which they had received from their Risen Lord.

The *word of God* is entrusted to them. It is a holy burden and a sacrosanct responsibility. "You shall be my witnesses" (1:8) —this legacy of the Lord was their bounden duty. "Woe is me, if I do not proclaim the gospel," writes Paul in his first letter to the Corinthians (9:16). And how great a priority this preaching of the gospel enjoyed is attested to in a surprising passage in the same letter: "Christ sent me not to baptize but to proclaim the good news of salvation " (1 Cor. 1:17). *Prayer* was equally an important part of the ministry of the word—as equally important a task as preaching; and not only personal prayer, such as Jesus himself had practiced for their imitation and had also impressed so strongly upon his apostles, but also and chiefly the prayer service in and with the community. Proclamation of the word of God and liturgical prayer are consequently the essential task of the apostles and compel them to overcome any and all obstacles which might prevent them from wholly fulfilling this, their vocation.

An earnest admonition is incorporated into their words: *an instruction and a regulation for all priestly and ecclesiastical service.* How easily the essentials of ministry are shrouded over and obstructed by secondary matters! For it is not always easy to ascertain what is essential and to safeguard it when one is pressed by the routine of daily duties and demands—and also when one encounters differences of opinion and temperament. We see this fully realized in the case of Paul when he "works" as a tentmaker (18:3) to earn a livelihood for himself and for his companions (20:33ff.). And when he mentions " daily pressure " and " solicitude for the churches " (2 Cor. 11:28), he intimates to us the multiplicity of cares which could and did actually affect him.

When the apostles endeavor to get down to essentials, they do not overlook a solution for the problem of the charitable tasks which face the community. They are concerned about *their co-workers and their helpers.* It was, consequently, a decision of far-reaching importance. They make their selection after they had asked for and received the cooperation of the entire community. The " twelve "—they are deliberately addressed as such—knew what their office was and also what rights were joined to it, namely, the right to guide and to make decisions. On the other hand, they were conscious of the dignity and the co-responsibility of the community. So from the beginning they tried to avoid creating the impression that the church was the affair of only those to whom the duty of guidance had been granted. The shibboleth of a " clericalized church " represents, consequently, an unhappy development which the church has repeatedly disavowed, because she has always been (or tried always to be) preoccupied with the task of self-renewal.

If the apostles demand *certain qualifications* in those to be chosen, they are prompted by that solicitude with which the church is at all times animated, when she calls men for the work of the holy ministry. Anyone who is conversant with the letters to Timothy and Titus knows of the demands which are made of those who are candidates for ecclesiastical office, whether they be bishops, priests, or deacons. " They should have a good reputation," it is stated; and this means they must enjoy the respect of the people as well as a good name. At the same time they should be " full of wisdom." The ministry makes it mandatory that candidates possess not only natural intelligence and talent, but also that wisdom which in the profoundest sense of the word wells up from out the mystery of the Holy Spirit.

The community is asked to name *seven* men from among their number. Why precisely seven? This number has become a definite symbol. In 21 : 8 we realize this best when the " evangelist " Philip is introduced to the Philippians as " one of the seven." The number seven has a significance which approximates that of the number twelve. Both numbers enjoy special status in the ancient world. In the Bible we encounter the number seven as a mysterious symbol, beginning with the seven-day week of the creation narrative down to the seven series in the Book of Revelation.

⁵*This proposal met with the approval of the entire community and they chose Stephen, a man filled with faith and the Holy Spirit, and Philip, Prochorus, Nicanor, Timon, Parmenas, and Nicholas, a proselyte from Athens.*

The community chooses its candidates. We can learn nothing about the way it actually took place. The situation is different from that which obtained at the election of Matthias (1 : 15ff.). The narrative creates the impression that the whole business was transacted at a single session, although we can assume that because of the tension existing between the Hellenists and the Hebrews at least several minor meetings had taken place prior to the plenary session. In his own narrative Luke compresses the results of what had transpired into this simple account. It was a memorable occasion. It becomes increasingly evident that the church as a *visible* institution is thrust into the everyday life of men and as such is in need of a well-ordered system of government.

The list of names has been subjected to careful scrutiny. The *names* which appear *are exclusively Grecian.* Does this possess any special significance? Without doubt. It is true that we also find in the list of the original twelve such Greek names as Andrew and Philip and in addition that of Peter, who received this Greek surname to replace the Aramaic, Cephas. The close ties existing between Judaism and Hellenic culture are demonstrated by these Greek names among the apostles. This does not, however, force us to call those apostles with Grecian names Hellenists. But since the names of the seven chosen by the community are all of Grecian origin, we may be permitted to conjecture that the voters did this to please the Judeo-Christian Hellenists and to heal any dissension which they might have foreseen in the offing. It is a question of church unity, of a blessing which was of decisive importance for the work of the future.

Are we to suppose that these seven Hellenists would serve the entire community? Or were they provided merely to look after the needs of the Hellenist group? Various opinions have been proposed on this point in numerous commentaries, but all of them are unfounded. One thing, however, becomes apparent, a matter necessary for the future development of the church, namely, that the Hellenist group retained its own identity in the community; in addition, it possessed *a progressive spirit* which later on would produce that tension which would explode into the persecution of the Christians. In this connection we may wish to recall the note in 8:1, according to which the apostles —and with them the Hebrew segments of the community—were ordered not to leave Jerusalem during the persecution.

⁶These they presented to the apostles, who praying over them laid their hands upon them.

Although the Greek text is neither clear nor univocal, we may, however, conclude that it was the apostles who laid their hands upon the men chosen by the community. For before the election, the apostles admonished the people, " Look around for seven men . . . these we shall appoint for this service " (6:3). *A law of the ecclesiastical hierarchy* is promulgated; it is put into almost legal terms. The apostles received their mission and their power from Christ; they in turn will pass them on to others, and in this way both the mission and the power will continue to exist in a never-ending succession, until the church will be absorbed into the consummation of the kingdom of God. " Built upon the foundation of the apostles and the prophets " is a description of the church in the words of Paul, " and its chief cornerstone is Jesus Christ. In him the entire structure is being closely fitted together and will grow into a holy temple dedicated to the Lord " (Eph. 2:20).

This law is all-comprehensive; it pervades the entire structure of the church, so that the invisible work of the Holy Spirit is intimately joined to the church's outer forms and institutions, which rest upon the foundation of the apostles. Of course, the *free activity of the Holy Spirit* will in no sense be pent up within such forms and institutions. Anyone who weighs well the call of Paul is conscious of this fact. The very earliest witnesses of tradition demonstrate, however, the care with which the church tried to preserve unbroken the line of succession by which ecclesiastical powers could be traced back to the mission of the apostles.

By the prayer and by the imposition of hands the apostles commissioned the seven, who had been chosen by the community, for the service of the church. Are we to see in these rites the administration of the sacrament of order? Or should we refrain from asking such questions and be content with the statement that the ones thus commissioned felt themselves justified and empowered to exercise their ministry? The imposition of hands is a primitive rite by which special power and jurisdiction have always been imparted. Moses is supposed to have laid his hands on Josue (Num. 27:18). In like fashion it is cited as a dictum of God: " Put something of your honors upon him, so that all the congregation of the Israelites may obey him " (Num. 27:20).

⁷The word of God continued to spread, and the number of

disciples grew greatly, and a great number of priests also accepted the faith.

With special care it is noted that included among the newly converted there were *many Jewish priests*. Even Jesus found disciples among these leaders of the people. As a result the evangelist was compelled to remark, " Because of the Pharisees, they did not openly profess their faith, lest they be put out of the synagogues, for they preferred the esteem of the people more than the approval of God " (Jn. 12:42f.). We may assume that the priests who became Christians still continued to perform the duties connected with their priestly office during their various turns in the temple. For the community of Christians was still intimately bound up with synagogal regulations and order, though their conversion made it very apparent that the church was steadily growing apart.

Stephen (6:8—8:3)

His Blessed Labors and His Persecution (6:8–14)

⁸Stephen, full of grace and of power, performed great miracles and signs among the people. ⁹Then, certain persons who belonged to the so-called Synagogue of the Freedmen, Cyrenians, and Alexandrians and those from Cilicia and, Asia rose up and argued with Stephen. ¹⁰They were, however, unable to withstand the wisdom and the Spirit with which he spoke.

Just as Peter the apostle had hitherto occupied an important place and had labored within the community, so now *Stephen* steps forward from out among the seven and enters the foreground of the narrative, though what is related of him resembles in many respects the deeds of the apostle Peter. Just as "the wonders and signs" of the apostles are stressed (2:44; 5:12), so these same portents are ascribed to Stephen and later to Philip (8:6). *Grace and power* were his peculiar gifts. And these phrases paraphrase the fullness of the gifts of the Holy Spirit with which the infant church was able to prove her identity as a work of salvation perfected by God.

To the testimony "in wonders and signs" is added *the word-breathing Spirit,* by which Stephen is directed to devote his energies to that group among the Jews which up to that moment had not been so directly addressed: that is, to the Hellenist Jews, even though we have already seen and heard of this faction in the then existing community on at least one other occasion; and even though it was from this circle that there arose grievances and complaints against the neglect being shown in the care of widows. But ever since men of Hellenist origin, possessing as they did special gifts, had taken up a place alongside the twelve, it appears that this had prepared the way for an extremely lively exchange of ideas within the Hebrew coterie.

By this interlude we are also made aware of another forward step of the church in her outward development. *Theological discussions* relative to the Christian message of salvation are now brought out into the open. From the testimony of the disciples and of the apostles, from the proclamation of salvation which is shown to be in agreement with the scriptures, there grows in closest *rapprochement* with Hellenism endeavor to fathom more profoundly the mystery of the revelation of Christ and to establish the great cohesion and the complete correlation of salvation history. The magnificent speech of Stephen before the Sanhedrin furnishes us with an example of this tendency. The Acts of the

Apostles points out with special emphasis the inherent power of the infant church, when it speaks of the triumphal nature of the " Spirit and of the wisdom " with which Stephen proclaims and demonstrates the veracity of the message of Christ.

¹¹Then they instigated certain men who alleged, " We have heard how he blasphemed against Moses and against God!" ¹²And they stirred up the people as well as the elders and ¹³the Scribes; they rushed upon him and brought him before the Sanhedrin. They produced false witnesses who claimed, " This man never ceases to speak against the Holy Place and the Law. ¹⁴We have heard him say, ' This Jesus of Nazareth will destroy this holy place and change the customs which Moses had handed over to us '."

Religious fanaticism and obstinacy utilize the most ineffectual kind of weapons: personal hatred and personal defamation. What Stephen encountered before the Council is simply a repetition of what Jesus had experienced in his struggle with Judaism, namely, tenaciousness to external tradition. What more in the way of base and distorted motives could these men have contrived to invent? In their felt-impotency they seized upon the most primitive weapons of warfare, and they were so biased that they showed no readiness to gather evidence and to arrive at an impartial knowledge of the truth. We know of the excuse they used to produce false witnesses in the trial of Jesus, a fact which is narrated by both Mark and Matthew. It is surprising that in his account of the trial of Jesus, Luke makes no mention of the false witnesses (Lk. 22:66). By this we are made apprised of the peculiarities of his literary style, namely, to avoid repeating similar or related incidents. It is assumed that he knew of the summoning and the appearance of false witnesses in the trial of Jesus from the gospel of Mark, which he most probably used as a source material. It is consequently of importance to him to be able to recount that the same kind of procedure was employed in the trial of Stephen.

Blasphemies against God and Moses are the charges which are alleged against Stephen. According to Judaic tradition, Moses is the father of the law. We know from the gospel how Jesus' accusers imputed to him the same transgressions against the law. The whole struggle of the Scribes against Jesus is based on this charge. One should read the Sermon on the Mount according to Matthew (Mt. 5–7) in order to understand Jesus' stand with regard to the law, when he repudiated the obdurate supremacy of the letter of the law and its external formulas and sought to make clear to his hearers what the true intention of the Spirit was. We know that the sentence of death was pronounced against Jesus by the Sanhedrin because of his supposed " blasphemy against God."

STEPHEN BEFORE THE SANHEDRIN (6:15—7:53)

[15]*All who sat in the Council turned their eyes upon him and saw that his face was like the face of an angel.*

Stephen stands before the Supreme Council of the Jews. The weightiest charges which could be made against a Jew have been brought against him. A tumultuous crowd had hauled him before the court—before the same court that had condemned Jesus to death and before which not so long ago the apostles had also stood, only to be freed after having been punished with lashes. What did the men of this court have in mind? The majority of them were swollen with hatred. But all were deeply concerned about this man. A light streamed from his face. *They saw that his face shone like that of an angel.* Was this really true? Or is the author of this account trying to place the " hero " of his tale in the limelight of the miraculous? We know something of the exaggerated and hyperbolic style of pious legends which show a decided preference for lifting an event above the drab details of everyday life to a plane where it will awaken in the reader sentiments of astonishment and wonderment.

Yet we have no convincing reason to question the veracity of this statement. May we not assume that the youthful Saul personally shared the experience or at least was able to verify it first-hand? In this way, Luke had received a credible report of the incident. Why should it be impossible for one so manifestly filled with the Holy Spirit as Stephen to be flooded by light of unusual brilliancy, which reflected the *majestic splendor of God*? Did not fire descend on Pentecost which affected the faithful present in a very perceptible way (2:3)? Was not an ineffable brilliance manifest at the transfiguration of Jesus (Lk. 9:29)? And are we not justified in surmising that the Risen One was suffused by a light supernatural in origin—even though he was capable of suppressing it at any moment he chose and had so chosen up to that moment? Was not Saul before Damascus irradiated by a lustrous brilliance from out of which our Lord addressed him?

The glowing countenance of Stephen appeared to be a *sign*— a sign especially for the Sanhedrin, but also a sign which the church in her hour of dire need required so desperately. Was not the young Saul perhaps even then—although he intended at the time to make the persecution of the Christians his life work— motivated by the memory of the event when he later described the glory of the apostles' service (2 Cor. 3:7ff.)? He recalls Moses: " whose service was performed in such a brilliancy, that the sons of Israel were not able to look upon his face because of the brilliancy which lighted up his countenance " (Ex. 34:29ff.). Of the ministry of the apostles Paul writes, " What once had splendor, has come to have no splendor at all in view of the splendor that surpassed it. For if what is transitory manifested itself in such splendor, what is permanent must radiate much more splendor " (2 Cor. 3:10ff.).

7:1Then the high priest spoke, " Is this so?" He replied, " Brothers and fathers, listen."

This is the introduction to one of the longest speeches in the whole Acts of the Apostles, and also one of the most original, from the standpoint of content. In this regard it also approximates the salvation-history presentation with which Paul begins his missionary sermon in Antioch, in Pisidia (13:16ff.). How are we to understand the speech of Stephen? Does it actually fit the situation into which it is inserted? Is it truly an answer to the question of the high priest? Is it—at least we would like to put the question—really the speech of a Christian or the salvation-historical sermon of a Jew? As far as content goes, the name of Jesus is mentioned only once, and then without using his actual name; and moreover only towards the end, when Stephen says, " They have murdered those who prophesied the coming of the Righteous One, whose betrayer and murderer you have now become " (7:52). Yet—to answer our question—the whole speech is indeed centered on Jesus, if we take Stephen's words in their most profound sense.

2b" The God of glory appeared to our father, Abraham, as he was staying in Mesopotamia, before he shifted to Haran ³and said to him: ' Leave this land and your relatives and go into the land which I will show you' (Gen. 12:1). ⁴Then he departed from the country of the Chaldees and settled in Haran, and from there after the death of his father, God transferred him into this land in which you now dwell. ⁵He gave him no heritage in it, not even a foot of ground, but he promised him he would give it to him and to his descendants as their possession, although at the moment he was childless. ⁶God spoke to this effect: ' His descendants will live as aliens in a strange land; they will make them slaves and will mistreat them for four hundred years. ⁷The people, however, to whom they are slaves I will judge, said the Lord and then they will depart (Gen. 15:13f.) and they will worship me in this place' (Ex. 3:12). ⁸And he gave him the covenant of circumcision, and so he begot Isaac, whom he circumcised on the eighth day, and so Isaac became the father of Jacob, and Jacob of the twelve patriarchs."

At the very beginning of the speech, we find two salvation-historical notions of importance: " the God of glory " and " Abraham, our father." The coupling of these names possesses a profound significance. The entire religious thought-processes of the Jews are based upon them. The pious faithful of the Old Testament bestowed the title " God of glory " upon their God. By this title, they paraphrased God's omnipotence, almightiness, holiness, wisdom, and incomparable perfection in contrast to which the gods of the heathens dwindle into insignificance. By this title they also bear witness to that ineffable glory which in accordance with Old Testament statements is part and parcel of the mysterious essence of God. This " God of glory " is found at the beginning of all human history; he preserves and guides it. It is he who makes himself accessible to his chosen people in a special manner. When Stephen places this God at the very beginning of his speech, he touches upon the holiest, the most sacrosanct possession of the people. In making a profession of faith in him, Stephen bears witness that this God is ever-present and is continuously determining, even in this fateful hour, when the Council is deliberating upon a most fateful problem. It is useful for an understanding of the speech to look carefully between the lines for thoughts which are otherwise not expressed. These will in turn lead us from the ancient salvation guidance of God to the new.

The history of this God begins for his people with Abraham. Thus an important historical statement is contained in Stephen's phrase, " Abraham, our father." Anyone who reads the New Testament writings carefully will learn something of the incomparable veneration which Abraham enjoyed in Jewish faith and thought. How important it is in the genealogy compiled by Matthew (1 : 1ff.) to establish that Jesus Christ is a son of Abraham! What pains Paul took in his Epistle to the Romans (4 : 1ff.) and in his Epistle to the Galatians (3 : 6ff. and 4 : 21ff.) to show that in Abraham the new work of salvation of God begins in Christ Jesus and to locate it within the context of salvation history! Abraham becomes " the father of all the faithful."

What does Stephen single out in the story of Abraham? He points out that the life of Abraham was a constant search and a constant wandering which he took upon himself as a task committed to him by God and performed in perfect obedience: from Mesopotamia to Haran, and from Haran to Palestine. How living there as an " alien " he received the promise of God concerning his descendants which at that moment he did not have and upon which he could not reckon. He lived entirely according to promise and the faith which it engendered. This is indeed the distinctive note which Stephen sought to recall to the minds of the Sanhedrin. By this he said, as it were without saying it, how this God consistently demanded constantly new acts of *faith and obedience,* whenever he reveals himself to men as all-powerful in their salvation.

⁹*" The patriarchs were jealous of Joseph and sold him into Egypt, but God was with him.* ¹⁰*He rescued him from all his afflictions, adorned him with grace and wisdom in the sight of Pharaoh, the king of Egypt, who made him ruler over Egypt and his whole household.* ¹¹*A famine came upon the whole of Egypt and Canaan, and our ancestors were unable to find any food.* ¹²*When Jacob heard that grain was available in Egypt, he sent our fathers there for the first time.* ¹³*On a second occasion Joseph revealed his identity to his brothers, and in this way Joseph's family became known to Pharaoh.* ¹⁴*Joseph sent his brothers back and had his father return with them, along with all his kindred, seventy-five souls in all.* ¹⁵*And Jacob went down to Egypt and died there, himself and our fathers.* ¹⁶*They were afterwards carried back to Sichem and placed in a grave which Abraham had purchased for a sum of silver from the sons of Hemor in Sichem."*

Another episode of Jewish history is portrayed as a history of God. *God was with him:* upon this phrase we must place the accent; it possesses a special significance. In this incident Joseph, son of Jacob, occupies the center of the stage. The main features of the story are known to us from Bible history. We know how Joseph was rescued from a dire fate and rapidly rose to become the liberator not only of the Egyptians who had exalted him but also of those who had sought to destroy him, his own brothers. By a special act of providence he thus becomes the founder of the people of God who gathered together around Jacob in Egypt to the number of seventy-five. Without anything being said about it, we can detect a veiled reference to the new people of God which was to be called into being by Jesus. Joseph was sold by his brothers and delivered over to the caravan of merchants (possibly slave dealers). God, however, rescued him from such a dreadful fate and permitted him to become the saviour of the very ones who had plotted against him.

Thoughts recalled from previous sermons of the apostles insinuate themselves here and help us to look at these Old Testament ideas with the eyes of the disciples of Jesus. Does the fact that Joseph reveals himself to his brothers only on the second visit contain some hidden significance? Should this not serve to remind us that Jesus will disclose himself only on his second coming in all his ineffable majesty? Would we do justice to the purpose of the speech if we drew the conclusion that in seemingly hopeless situations it is God alone who steers the course which leads to eternal life? What lesson should the Sanhedrin have drawn from the story of Joseph? The story itself had been known to them for a long time. Should it not have brought home to them the fact that they should be prepared to expect a saviour from God in a moment of dire distress for the Jewish nation? Could they not have understood Stephen's words in this sense? Or could not the story of Joseph, especially in its method of composition, have been conceived to convey the idea of introducing a still greater and more meaningful event which is so closely linked to the figure of Moses?

[17] " Now, when the time of the promise drew near, the promise

which God had made to Abraham, the people in Egypt increased and multiplied, ¹⁸until another king became lord of Egypt, who knew nothing of Joseph. ¹⁹He was filled with evil intent against our race and maltreated our fathers by forcing them to expose their new born children, so that they might not survive. ²⁰At this time Moses was born, and was the elect of God. For three months he was reared in the house of his father, but when he was exposed ²¹the daughter of Pharaoh adopted him and raised him as her own son. ²²Moses was instructed in all the wisdom of the Egyptians; he was eloquent of speech and mighty in strength."

The figure of Moses is now exhibited for our consideration; by far the greater part of the speech is devoted to this figure. Judaism considered him to be the founder of the civil, social, and religious institutions of the people. Since the entire conduct of Judaism is bound up with his name, it is important for Stephen and his interests that he present as an impressive picture of this man as possible. For was he not charged with disrespect for the law and for Mosaic tradition?

The very way in which the birth of Moses is depicted forces us to look beyond him to Jesus. " Now when the time of the promise drew near, the promise which God had made to Abraham, the people in Egypt increased and multiplied." The time had ripened for the *advent of the promise.* This thought is also expressed in the New Testament. In the " fullness of time " (Gal. 4:4) the new exodus arrives in the person of Jesus. Jesus himself introduces his message with the call to salvation: " The time is fulfilled and the kingdom of God is at hand " (Mk. 1:15). And when it is stated that " the time of the promise is near which God made to Abraham," there rings out that theology of promise which we find developed so definitively and so impressively in Paul. Is not the image of the enslaved chosen people in Egypt a symbol of the need for the salvation of mankind at the coming of Christ?

But we listen to all these things as Christians and from them we draw our conclusions. Stephen himself is aroused first of all by his review of Jewish history. We are all too prone to recall the preservation of the child Jesus as he fled from the murderous ordinance of Herod. Luke does not, however, describe this scene in his account of Jesus' childhood; but Matthew did. Are we permitted to supplement the speech of Stephen by incorporating into it these thoughts taken from Matthew? Are we justified in seeing in his statements concerning Moses, namely, that he was "eloquent of speech and mighty in strength," a relationship to those words which the disciples at Emmaus addressed to Jesus of Nazareth, that he was a "prophet, mighty in word and in deed before God and the whole people" (Lk. 24:19)?

[23]" When he reached the age of forty, it entered his mind to visit his brethren, the sons of Israel. [24]And he saw how one was being treated unjustly, he stepped in and avenged the one being wronged by striking down the Egyptian. [25]He assumed that his brothers would understand that God wished to save them through him. But they did not understand. [26]On the next day he approached them as two of them were quarreling together and he tried to restore peace by saying, 'Men, you are brothers! Why do you wrong each other?' [27]Then the one who had done the other an injustice pushed him aside and said, 'Who has placed you as ruler and judge over us? [28]But you perhaps want to kill me as you killed the Egyptian yesterday?' [29]Upon hearing this, Moses fled and settled down for a time as an alien in the land of Madian, where he begot two sons."

What Stephen relates of Moses was already well known to the Supreme Council from passages in the Book of Exodus (2: 12–14). Why does he repeat them again here? Had this anything to do with the accusations which had been alleged against him? Not directly. There was, nevertheless, something in it which the judges before whom he was arraigned had to hear. There is a sentence in his sermon upon which everything hinges. Moses " assumed that his brothers would understand that God wished to save them through him." But *they did not understand.* They did not accept Moses as *the saviour of his people.* Intentionally the sermon deals with " his brothers." He comes to them as one of their very own and tries to help them. Lack of understanding on their part drove him to seek refuge in a foreign land.

Certainly the recollection of these scenes taken from Israel's most miserable era must have forced the members of the Sanhedrin to consider them now at some length. Should not the accusers have acknowledged that the accused could claim with justice that he was being guided by a mandate from God? Should they not have recalled the counsel and the advice which Gamaliel had proferred, that same Gamaliel who had moved this same Council to restrain itself from dealing harshly with the apostles (5: 34ff.)? Can not we see in the image of Moses both concealed testimony and witness to another who was the *saviour of his people?* For this similarity with Jesus is indeed impressed upon us. Should we not take for granted that Stephen actually wished to speak of Jesus when he referred to Moses?

Was not Jesus, commissioned as he was to save his brothers, forced to suffer from the same lack of comprehension and from the same form of resistance that Moses met with? We are well acquainted with such scenes from the gospels. We recall, for example, the people of Nazareth who took exception to Jesus sermon on salvation, and drove him out of the city—an incident which Luke so graphically describes in his gospel (4:28ff.). We are reminded also of the Scribes and the Pharisees who asked with a sneer, " Who then is this who speaks so blasphemously?" (5:21). And was not Jesus often forced to take to flight to escape from the blows of his " brothers," exactly as Moses had?

*30"When forty years had passed, an angel appeared to him in the flames of a burning thorn bush in the desert of Mount Sinai. *31Moses looked with wonderment at the sight, but when he approached close to see more clearly, he was permitted to hear the voice of the Lord, *32' I am the God of your fathers, the God of Abraham, Isaac, and Jacob.' Moses trembled and did not dare to look. *33Then the Lord spoke to him, ' Remove the sandals from your feet, for the place on which you are standing is holy ground. *34I have watched you and I saw my people mistreated in Egypt and I listened to their groaning and have come down to deliver them. And now come, I wish to send you to Egypt'."*

A great veneration for Moses pervades these words. Stephen was also conversant with the divine mystery which Moses encountered. He also knew of the task with which he was entrusted. In such circumstances was the charge made against him justified? How could he be capable of " blaspheming against Moses " and " against God "? May we not find in these statements about Moses certain hidden and implicit references to that One whose public ministry also began in the desert? Did not the voice of God the Father speak to Jesus as he prepared to enter upon the work of redeeming his people? For he was enabled to become aware of the revelation and his choice by God: " You are my beloved son in whom I am well-pleased "

(Lk. 3:22). Thus a mysterious encounter with God is found at the beginning of the story of both saviours—and it appears as if the speech of Stephen fully intended to turn our attention to these similarities.

[35]" *This Moses whom they had disowned, saying: ' Who has placed you as ruler and a judge over us?'—him God sent back as a ruler and a deliverer with the help of the angel who had appeared to him in the thorn bush.* [36]*He led them out with the help of Egypt and in the Red Sea and in the desert for forty years.* [37]*He is the Moses who said to the sons of Israel, ' The Lord your God will raise up a prophet from among the brethren as he did me'* (Deut. 18:15). [38]*This is he who was the mediator for his people in the desert between the angel who spoke to him on Mount Sinai and our fathers. He received the oracles of life, in order to give them to us.*"

With good reason it has been said that in these sentences, which represent the climax of the witness concerning Moses, we can detect a hymn in which in an exalted form the grandeur of Moses is given full expression. Precisely by these words Stephen impressively refutes the accusation that he " blasphemed both God and Moses." For his words are a moving as well as a compelling profession of faith in the ruler and the deliverer of the Jewish people. He sees in him a person called personally by God through the medium of an angel. Stephen is also conscious of the charism of miracles which Moses exercised while the Jews were leaving Egypt, of his charism of prophecy with which, peering into the future, he spoke of that other prophet whom God would raise up. Stephen then recalls the mediatorship of Moses in those powerfully moving salvific scenes

on Mount Sinai and in the legislation which since then has in
Judaism been inseparably linked with the name of Moses.
Instead of being an enemy of the Mosaic covenant—the charge
with which he has been accused—Stephen is rather fully cognizant of the law dating back to Moses, for as he says, " He received the *oracles of life,* in order to be able to give them to you."

With this definitive description of the law Stephen reaches
back to the Book of Leviticus where the Lord admonishes Moses
thus: " You shall, therefore, keep my statutes and my commandments; whoever acts according to them, he shall live by
them " (18:5). We are also reminded of the words which Jesus
used to answer the man who asked him, " What must I do to
obtain eternal life?" Jesus replied, " If you would enter into
eternal life, keep my commandments." And then Jesus repeated
for his benefit the commandments which derive from Mosaic
law (Mt. 19:17ff.)

We finally return again to the question which has troubled us
all along and has been on our minds all through Stephen's
speech. Does Stephen say all of this simply to extol Moses and
his law? Does he not again speak here, in cryptic language, of
another for whom Moses is the counterpart in salvation history,
of a new Moses, of Christ Jesus? In these statements are we not
aware of the invisible presence of the true " ruler and saviour "?
Do not the " wonders and the signs " which are ascribed to
Moses also indicate those " powerful deeds, wonders, and signs "
by which Jesus of Nazareth was accredited (2:22ff.). Are not the
departure from Egypt and the subsequent journey through the
desert a symbol of these deeds by which Jesus led the *new people
of God* from out their sinfulness and loss of grace to " everlasting life "?

And does this not hold true of the word of the Deuteronomist, which is without doubt the most powerful statement in Stephen's whole speech, namely, that " The Lord, your God, will raise up a prophet from among the brethren as he did me " (Deut. 18 : 15)? Should not these pregnant phrases have prompted the members of the Sanhedrin to pause and to ponder their predicament? They did not need to be told about what had actually happened to all of those who bore witness to Jesus of Nazareth. Certainly they recalled the " oracles " of Peter (4 : 9ff.; 5 : 29ff.), so that they could not have been mistaken about what Stephen wished to tell to them when he quoted the prophetic words of Moses. We recall also how these same words were referred to Jesus by Peter, when, after healing the man born lame, he addressed the people: " Thus Moses spoke: ' The Lord, our God, will raise up for you a prophet from among your brothers, as he did me. You must listen to him in all things whatever he will say to you. But it shall, however, be so: everyone who does not listen to this prophet shall be destroyed from among the people " (3 : 22ff.). When we further recall that in the presence of Moses these same words again fill the air at the time of the transfiguration of Jesus (Mk. 9 : 7), we cannot but feel that they had a special significance in the apostolic preaching of Jesus.

When Stephen speaks of the " oracles of life," he might first of all have thought of the Jewish law; but the phrase itself impels us to recall the admonition of the angel, who had liberated the apostles from prison and had then warned them: " Go, put in an appearance in the temple and proclaim to the people all the words of this life " (5 : 20). It is scarcely a matter of chance that twice within such a short space of time express mention is made of the " oracles of life." Thus the Acts of the Apostles expressly permits us to hear the message of the new Moses, though veiled in the literal meaning of Stephen's speech

—yet a veil which the Sanhedrin could scarcely have failed to see through.

³⁹" *Our fathers refused to be subject to him, so they thrust him aside and turned back in their hearts to Egypt, saying to Aaron,* ⁴⁰' *Make us gods, who may go before us; as for this Moses who has led us out of the land of Egypt—we do not know what has happened to him*' (Ex. 32:1, 23). ⁴¹*And in those days they made for themselves an image of a calf, sacrificed to the idol and took delight in the work of their hands."*

Stephen reviews one of the most sorrowful chapters in Israelite history. Those who had hauled him before the court, where they had charged him with blasphemy against Moses, were forced now to recall that in the past " their fathers " had rebelled against their ruler and saviour and that by their adoration of the Egyptian calf they had *turned away from God* and plunged into idolatry. Of what had they accused Stephen? " We have heard that he blasphemed against Moses and against God," claimed the witnesses whom they had summoned and haggled over. And of what wrongdoing were their fathers guilty? They, too, had revolted against Moses and God.

⁴²" *God turned away from them and abandoned them to the worship of the host of heaven, as it is written in the Book of the Prophets,* ' *Did you not offer to me sacrifices and sacrificial victims for forty years in the desert, house of Israel? You have the tent of Balaam along with you, the star of the god, Rephab, the images which you made to adore them. Therefore, I will cause you to go into captivity beyond Babylon* ' " (Amos 5:25ff.).

The obstinate people experience the punishment foretold by God.

God turned away from them. We perceive what is meant when we consider what the presence of God meant in the religious thinking of the Old Testament. Israel knew that she was the favored child of God. Self-consciously and triumphantly the Israelites surveyed the idolatry of the people who surrounded them. The pureness and the uniqueness of their notion of God were a privilege as well as a characteristic of Israelitic history. It was a chaotic picture of idolatry with which Israel was faced. The history of religion bears this out in antiquity. It is also testified to by the men of God in the Old Testament who in their speeches express zeal for the one true God in frightening words.

[44]*" Our fathers had in the desert the tent of witness in accordance with the ordinance of him who spoke to Moses, that he should build it according to the model which he had examined.* [45]*Our fathers inherited it and under Josue brought it with them when they occupied the territory of the heathens, whom God had driven out before our fathers, up to the days of David.* [46]*But the Most High does not dwell in what is made by hands, as the prophet says:* [49]*" The heavens are my throne, the earth my footstool. What kind of a house do you wish to build for me, says the Lord, or what is the place of my rest?* [50]*Has not my hand made all that? ' "*

Stephen now turns his attention to and begins to speak of that other " tent " which as a cultural sanctuary was the renowned center of Jewish worship. We know from the Book of Exodus with what care of detail the people fitted out and guarded this sacred object. *The temple* drew its inspiration and grew out of the tent of the covenant—the temple which Solomon constructed in such a fabulous fashion. One should read the psalms so as to become better acquainted with the religious ardor and pious enthusiasm which Judaism had for this holy sanctuary.

Stephen was accused of having said that " Jesus would destroy this temple " (6:14). This charge is similar to the one which Jesus' enemies tried to allege against him. In Mark the statements of the perjured witness are recounted. " We heard him say, I will destroy this temple made by hands and in three days build another not made by hands " (Mk. 15:58). In John these words are linked to the purging of the temple and clearly allude to Jesus' resurrection from the dead (Jn. 2:19). We also know that Jesus actually predicted the destruction of the temple; this has been handed down to us along with his speech on the last things.

The Jews jealously guarded the inviolability of their sanctuary. They dreamed of it as possessing an everlasting permanency. When they returned from the captivity, their first concern was to rebuild the house of the Lord that had been reduced to rubble and ruin. The Maccabees purified the temple that had been defiled and blessed it anew, and the anniversary of its purification was celebrated in the month of Kislev (Jn. 10:22). What does Stephen try to make clear about the accusation made against him concerning the temple? He knew the history of that venerable edifice, of the former tent of the covenant, of the plans of David, and of the edifice raised by Solomon. He also knew of the incomprehensible greatness of God of whose omnipotence *the temple was but a symbol.*

Stephen has the courage to refer to the prophet Isaiah, to that daring passage in which the limitations of all things earthly, even of the form and the manner of all *external worship of God,* are so boldly ridiculed and excoriated. Whatever man is able to build, in the final analysis it is the work of God. The temple in Jerusalem was numbered among the marvels of the ancient world, but when compared to divine majesty and power, which fill heaven and earth, it was like nothing.

⁵¹" *You stiff-necked and uncircumcised of heart and of ears! You always resist the Holy Spirit; as your fathers did, so do you likewise!* ⁵²*Which one of the prophets did not your fathers persecute? Yes, they killed those who foretold the coming of the Just One, of whom you have now become the betrayers and murderers.* ⁵³*You have received the law delivered by the angels, but you have not observed it.*"

With surprising harshness Stephen moves from his review of the past to a sharp attack against his accusers and his judges. It literally bursts from his lips, seemingly without any real motive prompting it. But whoever has understood Stephen's previous veiled references to the present will understand that now the moment has arrived to reveal the true motives behind the accusation, because the emotions of the witnesses for Christ are now aroused, and the masks of spurious piety, of counterfeit zeal for the law have been torn from the faces of the judges. Thus Stephen calls the members of the Supreme Council *stiff-necked* and *uncircumcised of heart and ears.* He consciously employs the figurative language with which the prophets of the Old Testament scourged the unapproachableness and the callousness of the people. " Circumcise yourselves to the Lord and remove the foreskin from your hearts, you people of Judah and inhabitants of Jerusalem. . . . Behold, you have uncircumcised ears; and they are incapable of understanding " (Jer. 4:4; 6:10).

Stephen brands the members of the Sanhedrin " betrayers and murderers " of the Righteous One. This is the harshest indictment that is made against those responsible for the crucifixion, and the harshest we encounter in the Acts up to this point. We may recall the words which Peter used on this score in his sermon on Pentecost (2:23, 36)—his accusation levelled at the Jewish people on the occasion of the healing of the man born lame (3:14). Twice previously the Supreme Council was compelled to listen to public rebuke by the apostles in connection with the Council's guilt for the death of Jesus. "Jesus Christ" whom "you have crucified," testified Peter at his first hearing (4:10). "Jesus, whom you hung upon the cross and whom you killed," declared Peter and the apostles at their second trial (5:30). And now Stephen makes the same charge and levels the most provocative accusation which a defendant could possibly formulate against a court; he declares that the Sanhedrin had betrayed and murdered the Righteous One.

Stephen had been indicted as one guilty of the crime of blasphemy against Moses and God, and had been brought to trial on these counts. He answers the allegation by submitting a cross-petition against the very tribunal which is trying him. "You have received the law delivered by the angels, but you have not observed it." The legislation to which he makes reference here is the Mosaic law. "Delivered by the angels" meant that the law was passed down through Moses to the Jewish people. The Scribes saw in such angelic cooperation a mark of distinction for and a glorification of the law itself. Yet Paul on the same ground, namely, the presence of the angel, tries to prove the subordinate position and the inferior nature of the law (Gal. 3:19).

"You have not observed the law." What did Stephen mean by this surprising attack against the supreme authority of the Jews? Is it not in itself an insult deserving of death? To what

extent did the Council's members fail to keep the law? Did he
mean the same transgression of the law which is described so
precisely in the letter to the Romans, where Paul says to the
Jews, " You boast of the law, but you dishonor God by breaking
it " (2:23)? Or may we understand by the term " law " the
whole revelation of the Old Testament, with its forward-looking
in the prophecies and its preparations for the coming of the
Christ, upon which Judaism prided itself without yet considering
them seriously? If this were the case, we would then arrive at
the same conclusion which can be found in the gospel of John,
when Jesus replies to the Jews: " Did not Moses give you the
law? And yet not one of you lives up to it " (Jn. 7:19). Or
perhaps we could ponder on another statement of Jesus: " You
search the scriptures, because you believe that in them you have
eternal life; and it is they who bear witness to me, but you refuse
to approach me that you might have life. . . . Do not think that
I will accuse you to the Father; *Moses is your accuser,* in whom
you have placed your hope. For if you really believe Moses, you
would also believe me; for he has written of me " (Jn. 5:39f, 45).

His Testimony in Blood (7:54–60)

*54When they heard this, they became furious and gnashed their
teeth against him. 55But he, filled with the Holy Spirit, looked
up to heaven, saw the glory of God, and Jesus standing at the
right hand of God, 56and he cried out, " I see the heavens
opened and the Son of man standing at the right hand of God."
57Then they cried out in a loud voice, stopped their ears, and fell
upon him. 58aThen they cast him outside the city and stoned
him.*

Stephen had been accused of the most heinous crimes: disdain for the Mosaic Law; blasphemy against God. With unparalleled boldness he hurls the same accusations at his accusers. He imputes to them the *very same crime* for which he himself is indicted, namely, that they themselves have not kept the law. He taxes them with the *betrayal and the murder* of him who gives meaning to and is the content of the whole of revelation. We can, humanly speaking, understand the ire of the councillors, who still pride themselves on their power and their responsibility to the people. Honorable and dishonorable motives are thus mixed together in their rage against Stephen. The same hectic emotionalism was evident at the trial of Jesus by the same Sanhedrin.

Nevertheless, this brave disciple, under grave threat, offers irrefutable witness to him to whom he had through faith professed allegiance. Stephen had spoken of " the God of glory." Now God bears witness to *his own presence*. What a striking and moving image! In the sight of his enraged accusers and judges, Stephen sees the heavens opened. " He saw the glory of God and Jesus standing at his right." The Holy Spirit had taken possession of his soul; and another world is opened before his very eyes. His profession of faith rings joyously throughout the hall. " Behold, I see the heavens opened, and the Son of man standing at the right hand of God."

Of one thing we can be sure: Stephen was hauled to his death, not so much because of his speech against the temple and the law, but because of his lucid profession of faith in Christ Jesus. And his witness concerning the vision of the transfigured Son of man, which unmistakably recalls the words of Jesus before the Sanhedrin, enkindled anew the councillors' hatred of him whom they had condemned to the cross because of blasphemy. This Jesus of Nazareth renewed his own death in that of Stephen's, as he will also later on many times, when he will again and again be hauled before courts countless times in the numberless scores of persons who confess in his name. Stephen is scheduled to die as a martyr of Christ. Through him the title " martyr," which originally meant simply " witness " by reason of its basic meaning in Greek, receives a special signification, namely, a witness who pays for his testimony to Christ by his blood and by his life.

⁵⁸ᵇ*The witnesses placed their garments at the feet of a young man named Saul.* ⁵⁹*And they stoned Stephen, as he prayed: " Lord Jesus, receive my spirit."* ⁶⁰*And falling upon his knees he cried out in a loud voice, " Lord, do not hold this sin against them!" Saying these words, he fell asleep.*

Verse 58 is peculiarly inserted into the text at this point. The witnesses who had charged the accused before the Sanhedrin were, according to Jewish custom, required personally to cast the first stone upon the condemned man. Jesus alluded to this custom in the narrative of the woman taken in adultery, when he said, " He who is without sin among you, let him cast the first stone " (Jn. 8:7). The outer garments of which the witnesses had divested themselves were guarded by a young man by the name of Saul. What is so important about this young man? We are, of course, acquainted with him. Had he not been named Saul, Luke would scarcely have mentioned either him or his presence at the stoning. He is, however, the man who will exert a great influence not only on the life of Luke, but also on the career of the whole church. Soon his image, exhibited here so very briefly, will later on assume sharper definition and will become more clearly defined, until in the concluding chapters he will completely and exclusively fill the pages of the Acts of the Apostles.

The stoning of Stephen was for Saul a *memorable encounter with the church*. It imprinted itself indelibly on his mind. Twenty years later he will confess to the Lord who appeared to him in Jerusalem, " As the blood of your witness, Stephen, was poured out, it was I who was present and approved and tended the garments of those who killed him." What meaning did this event have for Saul? He was no doubt one of those who not long before had quarreled so passionately with Stephen because of the novel teaching he proposed; and his impetuous heart still glowed with fanatical zeal for Jewish orthodoxy, as he confessed in his letter to the Galatians (Gal. 1:14). Yet we do not know whether or not at the time of Stephen's death, tinder was sparked in Saul's soul which was later to be fanned into a mighty flame by the grace of God until he finally was consumed by it in his own martyrdom as " a servant of Jesus Christ."

In such a context the prayer of Stephen for his enemies is not a sign of weakness combined with resignation, but rather the outward manifestation of a tremendous faith in the presence of God, reverential fear of the Holy Spirit, who alone can strengthen man *to conquer himself out of love for this God*. Only one who knows the innermost motive of the Son of God dying on the cross for a sinful world can hope to experience the true depth of the prayer of the blood-witness of Christ that has been poured out for all.

OUTBREAK OF THE PERSECUTION (8:1-3)

¹*Saul had given his consent to the death. On that same day there*

broke out a severe persecution against the community in Jeru-salem and all, with the exception of the apostles, were scattered throughout the region of Judea and Samaria. ²God-fearing men buried Stephen and made great lamentation over him. ³Saul, however, was harassing the community, forcing his way into their homes, dragging away men and women, and putting them in prison.

Is it not curious how closely *Saul* is linked in this narrative with the story of *Stephen*? Three times his name is mentioned soon after that of Stephen. He was just named as the custodian of the garments of those who did the stoning; now his consent to the death itself is stressed; and in the next sentence save one he appears as the persecutor of the church. No doubt Luke was trying to bring some kind of literary order to the various events which led to the further development of the church, for in these pithy sentences we are also given an intimation of what is to come. Furthermore, we have an indication as to how the per-secution of the church is intimately coupled to her growth and her strengthening. She receives strength and life for her fruitful development from the death and blood of Stephen. The first martyr was carried to his grave, and the youthful Saul, who had collaborated in his death, will soon be permitted to experience what he himself " must suffer for the name of Jesus " (9:16).

The stoning of Stephen denotes a significant stride forward in the history of the church. *Life springs from death.* We are reminded of these profoundly meaningful words of Jesus which he uttered as his own death approached ever closer: " The hour is come for the Son of man to be glorified. Amen, amen, I say to you, unless the grain of wheat falls into the ground and dies, it remains alone; but if it dies, it brings forth much fruit "

(Jn. 12:23f.). And we should also meditate on the words of Paul:
" For the sake of Christ, I am content with weakness, with in-
sults, with hardships, with persecutions, and with calamities; for
when I am weak, then I am strong " (2 Cor. 12:10). And again
we are made conscious of that mystery of the church which guides
and fills everything and brings external weakness in the view of
the world to interior victory: the mystery of the Holy Spirit.
Only with the active cooperation of this Spirit was it possible for
Stephen to see the heavens open and to behold the glory of God,
even as the stones were showering upon him from the infuriated
mob.

Philip (8:4–40)

IN SAMARIA (8:4–13)

[4]*Those, however, who were scattered, passed through the
countryside and preached the word of God. [5]Philip went down
to the chief city of Samaria and proclaimed to its people the
message of Christ. [6]Crowds of people paid close attention to what
he said, and listened in complete accord and witnessed the signs
which he worked. [7]For the unclean spirits departed with loud
outcries and many who were possessed, and many paralyzed and
lame were healed. So great joy reigned in that city.*

Just as a stormy wind disperses seed over the countryside, so the
persecution drove the faithful over the whole of Palestine, not
as forlorn waifs and people gone astray, but as ambassadors and
witnesses of life and preachers and bearers of salvation. The
" good news " of the " word " accompanied them. Inflamed

by the fire of the Spirit they became torchbearers of the Divine Flame. A basic and underlying concept of the Acts can be perceived in this sentence, structurally so simple. Opposition and persecution are unable to destroy the life-power of the church; on the contrary, the church grows and develops precisely in those moments when she is threatened and assailed the most. The presence of the Holy Spirit is visible when danger is the greatest.

Next to Stephen, only one other of these first missionaries, namely, Philip, is especially mentioned. His name is for obvious reasons placed second in the list of the seven (6:5). Later on the Acts will narrate that on his return from the third missionary journey with Paul, Philip became acquainted with Luke in Caesarea. In this way Luke was enabled to gather from him many interesting and worthwhile details concerning the infant church and also concerning Philip himself and the labors he performed on behalf of the gospel. In verse 21:8 we read, " The next day we went on further, arrived at Caesarea, and entered the home of Philip, the evangelist, who was one of the seven, and stayed with him. He had four daughters, all virgins, who were gifted with prophecy."

Finally, *great joy reigned in that city.* This sentence adds to our image of the church. The " good news " engenders *joyous sentiments* in the people. Even in the earliest statements concerning the primitive community this joyous attitude prevailed, as we have seen. Thus the faithful came together " in joy and purity of heart " (2:46). The man born lame was gripped by this sentiment as he ran and jumped about in the temple after his cure, praising the goodness and the omnipotence of Almighty God. Even the apostles were so affected when they were " found worthy to suffer dishonor for the sake of the name of Jesus " (5:41). Joy is one of the characteristics of the early church. It is an essential lineament of true Christianity, insofar as Christianity is a true encounter with God and a genuine experience of salvific grace imparted by the Holy Spirit.

⁹A man by the name of Simon had previously been in the city and had amazed the people of Samaria with his magical feats, since he had passed himself off as a " Great Man." ¹⁰From the smallest to the most influential all had made themselves dependent upon him and they maintained: " This man is the power of God, whom we call The Great." ¹¹They clung to him because he had for such a long time amazed them by his magical prodigies.

The messenger of the gospel encounters in Samaria a practitioner of magic, an art widespread in the ancient world. By the testimony of history and by the documents that have been preserved, we know how deeply the people were under the spell of magicians and of the magical arts which were practiced in a variety of forms. In this particular passage, even the Acts of the Apostles complements the data already extant for such a woeful human state of gullibility. On his very first missionary journey Paul encounters a " Jewish magician and false prophet by the name of Bar-Jesus " (13:6), also called " Elymas " (13:8). How influential and powerful magic was in Ephesus we learn also in 19:17, where the value of books so freely tossed into a bonfire was estimated at about fifty thousand drachmas.

It is not stated in what the magical prowess of the magician consisted. Since he had passed himself off as " great "; and since the people saw the " power of God " present in him because he paraded as the " Great One," we gain the impression that Simon possibly lay claim to a *messianic mission*. It is not at all clear whether he based his pretensions on Judeo-biblical notions or whether he drew them from Hellenic sources. In religious matters Samaria represented a syncretic mixture of religions, so the message of the gospel was scattered over a field truly ripe for the harvest.

¹²*When they professed their faith in Philip's message of the kingdom of God and the name of Jesus, they were baptized, men as well as women.* ¹³*In fact, Simon himself believed and was baptized, and attached himself to Philip and was amazed when he personally saw the great signs and wonders being worked.*

The Samaritans succumbed to the gospel. Two notions brought about their change of heart: the kingdom of God and the name of Jesus Christ. By design the contents of the message were designated as those of the " evangelists " (21:8). Both are inseparably connected with the " good news " preached by the nascent church. The *kingdom of God* or, as it might be translated, *the kingship* or the *lordship of God,* was a basic theme in the teaching of Jesus himself. The notion is especially common in the synoptic gospels, though John employs it as well. " The kingdom of God is at hand " (see Mk. 1:15) is a phrase which is repeated frequently in the message which Jesus delivered. While delivering it, he looks up to his heavenly Father, whose kingdom must be fashioned from among those who accept his will and do it here below.

Certain scholars see Jesus only as another who preached the kingdom of God, and not as the One upon whom the preaching itself was centered. Precisely the Acts of the Apostles demonstrates repeatedly how the message of God's salvific will only then be properly understood when the " name of Jesus Christ " is given that prominence which it deserves. The people of Samaria, who received the message of Philip, were baptized in the " name of Jesus " (2 : 38). They recognized salvation in comparison to which everything faded into insignificance, even what had been offered them in the magic of Simon as " the great power of God."

" They were baptized, both men and women." Belief in Christ includes, according to the economy of salvation based on Christ, also a *baptism in Christ*. One conditions the other. This we perceived even in the story of Pentecost. Belief requires a sacral, legalistic, and sacramental expression in baptism, both as a symbol and as a salvation-mediating event. In this connection we should read chapter 6 of the Epistle to the Romans in order to obtain at least an approximation of the meaning of baptism in the primitive Christian community. In this passage we can formally discern, despite the simplicity of its form, the unprecedented rush of the people to baptism, for it is noted explicitly : " men as well as women." When women are mentioned specifically, we cannot help but recall that Samaritan woman who learned from Christ about the " living water " which would become " a spring welling up to eternal life " (Jn. 4 : 14). Even at that time their conversation revolved around the question of salvation and around a knowledge and believing affirmation of Jesus as the " saviour of the world " (Jn. 4 : 42).

The startling thing, however, is the fact that *Simon himself* disposed himself for belief in Christ and was baptized. To be sure, the motives behind his action are not suggested; but certainly did not spring from a yearning for salvation. We would like to be able to say that we could draw such a conclusion from the text itself, but his later attitude towards Peter supplies us with indications, if not actual proof, that his intentions were not genuine (8 : 18). Moreover, the judgment of the fathers is not at all favorable towards Simon in this regard.

The Imparting of the Holy Spirit by the Apostles (8 : 14–25)

[14]*When the apostles who were in Jerusalem heard that Samaria had received the word of God, they despatched to them Peter and John.* [15]*These went down and prayed for them so that they might receive the Holy Spirit.* [16]*For he had not as yet descended upon them; they had only been baptized in the name of the Lord Jesus.* [17]*Then they laid their hands upon them and they received the Holy Spirit.*

Here a very meaningful insight *into the essence of the church* is afforded us. The text itself depends greatly on the preceding excerpt. Anyone who reads with attention the lines which follow can scarcely overlook the fact that Simon Magus still dominates the narrative. Nevertheless, the peripheral notes, which we have reproduced in verses 14–17, are of far more importance for an understanding of the early church than are those passages devoted to Simon Magus.

Again the apostles appear on the scene. No matter how sharply the activities of the seven are projected, as this is done so graphically for us in the cases of Stephen and Philip, nevertheless everything is subordinated to the *authority of the apostles.* Their position and their plenipotentiary powers again receive added emphasis. Jerusalem is still the center from which they supervise the spread of the church. With utmost attention they follow the work of the messengers of the faith as they spread over the countryside.

For the twelve in Jerusalem belong to the *basic structure of the church*. The whole of the New Testament literature bears witness to this. In the course of the Acts of the Apostles we will be supplied further evidence. With full consciousness and in the fullness of his official commission, Peter visits the newly founded communities in Lydda and Joppe (9:32) so that he might be summoned from there to Caesarea for a decisive task which awaits him. Although the first gentile Christian community was in the throes of being established in Antioch the mother community in Jerusalem still felt responsible—without doubt under the guidance of the apostles—for what was happening and thus commissioned Barnabas to go there as its representative, endowed with all the necessary powers (11:22). And when in Antioch the first full-fledged quarrel arose over the unorthodox missionary methods of Paul and Barnabas, it was decided that " several of their members should go up to Jerusalem to the apostles and to the elders to consult about the question " (15:2).

The *authority of the apostles* is also accorded a prominent place in the case of Samaria, for example when Peter and John were despatched to there from Jerusalem. In Samaria it was a question of bearing witness to the *unity of the church,* of being concerned about unanimity both in doctrine and in morals, of seeing to the completion of what the messengers of faith had begun.

Again we are made conscious in this context of the primacy of Peter. Nor is it without significance that here again John accompanies Peter as his companion. Is he only a companion? Or does he share in the authority and the pre-eminence of Peter? These questions bear on a fundamental concern of the New Testament, namely, the structure of the church. Peter possesses—there can be no doubt—a position of precedence and special dignity in the college of the apostles. Many texts bear witness to this fact. But despite their frequency we gain the impression, and this is not seldom, that this primacy does not carry with it a rank distinct from that of the other apostles. His office as well as his pleni- tude of power are realized only in close cooperation with the other apostles. This is expressed in the passage we are now con- sidering.

It is worthwhile noting that Peter does not go alone but with John, and that John together with Peter labored with love in Samaria. It does not appear that Peter took John along with him, rather that *both were sent by the other apostles.* And even though from these circumstances we cannot draw any conclu- sions about the basic juridical relationships which existed among the apostles at the time, the fact is important for an understand- ing of the church. Later we shall examine the incident in Jeru- salem when Peter is forced to justify himself before the " apos- tles " and also before the brethren of Judea (11 : 11ff.), when he is questioned about his encounter with Cornelius, the gentile Roman centurion. In the office which Peter occupied, there seems to have been a tension between his undeniable primacy on the one hand and his affiliation with the other apostles and the entire community on the other. It required the constant presence of the Holy Spirit to make this tension fruitful in blessings for the church.

When both the apostles arrived in Samaria, they prayed for those whom Philip had baptized, so that the *Holy Spirit might descend upon them.* How are we to understand this? Did the apostles travel all the way from Jerusalem solely with this in mind? Or did they make the trip to fulfill this need only after the reception of the Holy Spirit? Actually the question in the final instance is concerned with a problem: whether those who had been baptized could have received the Holy Spirit without

their coming and without their laying on of hands. The sentence
has a strange ring about it: " He had not descended upon any
of them; they had only been baptized in the name of Jesus." Is
there or has there ever been a baptism in which the Holy Spirit
has not been conferred? We touched upon this question once
before in connection with the narrative of Pentecost (2:38). In
that connection we read the words of Peter: " Repent, and let
each of you be baptized in the name of Jesus Christ for the forgiveness of your sins, and you shall receive the power of the
Holy Spirit." We must realize that whatever the answer, the
mystery of the Spirit does not permit itself to be fitted into any
rigid, schematic category or order.

[18]*When Simon saw that the Spirit was bestowed by the laying-on
of the hands of the apostles, he offered them money* [19]*and said,
" Grant me also this power, so that any one upon whom I lay my
hands may receive the Holy Spirit."* [20]*Peter, however, said to
him, " May your money perish with you, because you think that
the gift of God may be acquired for money.* [21]*You have no part
and no right to this message; for your heart is not sincere in the
sight of God.* [22]*Do penance, therefore, for this your wickedness
and pray to our Lord that, if possible, he may forgive you the
desire of your heart.* [23]*For I can see that you are full of the gall
of bitterness and are held fast by the bond of iniquity."* [24]*Simon
replied, " Pray for me to the Lord, that he permit nothing of
what you have threatened."*

It becomes clear to anyone who reads these verses meditatively
that the bestowal of the Spirit by the apostles is being recounted
precisely because of the clash between Peter and Simon. It should
also become clear that this narrative concerning the laying-on of

hands is inserted between the two pericopes in which Simon
Peter is mentioned. The complete superiority of the apostles is
impressively portrayed for us in this encounter with the magician, a feature which appears frequently in the Acts of the
Apostles. At the same time the *questionableness of the conversion* of Simon is also clearly stressed. It has already been stated
in verse 13 that the magician was greatly impressed by the
" great signs and wonders " which Philip wrought; now it is
the extraordinary outpouring of the gifts of the Spirit which
evokes his interest. He lacks purity of heart and the living faith
which are conducive to salvation. He still fails to grasp the mystery of the Spirit. He continues to think and to calculate in terms
and practices of his magical craft. According to his own idea on
the matter, the apostles possess secret powers which are akin to
magic, and he strives to purchase them with money. Nothing is
said which would lead us to believe that he himself personally
wished to possess the Spirit; he is desirous of something else. He
tries to acquire the power of being able to transfer charisms and
powers to others. He is prepared to part with money in order to
reap money in return.

Let us again take a short backward glance at our passage.
" This man is the power of God, whom we call ' The Great ' "
(8: 10)—these are the words used by the Samaritans, amazed as
they were by the magical arts of Simon. Now the tremendously
greater power of God is brought forth in Samaria. This is
evidenced in the great deeds which Philip performs; this is
evidenced more strikingly and more provocatively in the revelation of the powers which the Holy Spirit possesses and exercises.
And the magician, who had previously shown himself to be so
astounded, is still more confounded by this power. He offers to
the apostles, who have these powers to be used at their discre-

tion, a sum of money to purchase this incalculable commodity of the Spirit. Ever since then the term " simony " reminds us of his proposal; it denotes every tainted, greedy, rapacious or underhanded bargaining for and dealing in spiritual goods.

We can readily understand the curse by which Peter stigmatizes this request. Almost automatically our thoughts run to that other encounter in which the devil tempted the Son of God and tried to turn him away from the course he was pursuing (Lk. 4: 1ff.). Even on that occasion it was material things which the devil sought to use in order to render Jesus pliable to his will. Peter speaks from the consciousness of his power, from the deepest recesses of his heart, as he did in the case of Ananias and Saphira, as we well know. So once more, the *office of Peter* must again be exercised, this time by watching and warning all of the inviolability of the spiritual goods confided to the church. For we know how the sin of a Simon will always try to find entry into the sanctuary and will try to dispose of the goods of the Holy Spirit to the common thief of greedy inclinations.

Harsh and sharp are the words which issue from the mouth of Peter. By them he expresses the same emotions which shook him when he stood before Ananias and Saphira. With similar passion in Cyprus, Paul inveighs against the sorcerer Elymas, who attempted " to make crooked the straight ways of the Lord " (13:9). When *truth and the sacral* are at stake, the church as a cherub with flaming sword is summoned to check the advance of whatever is unholy.

[25]*After they had given testimony and had proclaimed the word, they started back to Jerusalem and preached the gospel in many villages of the Samaritans.*

We know the literary genre of Luke. He shows a decided preference for coupling together individual stories and for taking a glance at the breadth and depth of the whole ensemble. He has hitherto been concerned with Samaria and the work of Philip; but he avails himself of every opportunity to bear witness everywhere to what had been entrusted to him. Later on Paul and Barnabas will on their way from Antioch to Jerusalem greet " their brethren " in Samaria and inform them of their success (15:3).

Conversion of the Official of Ethiopia (8:26–40)

The story which begins with 8:26 presents us with another example of the activity of the seven. Chapters 6–8 thus form a literary unit. For technical reasons, the author compresses together chronologically scattered bits of information with the result that we are unable to say with any degree of accuracy when Philip encountered the Ethiopian. Nor can we determine what time-relationship our story has to the content of the following chapter.

26Now an angel of the Lord spoke to Philip, and said, " Rise and proceed to the south on the road that goes down from Jerusalem to Gaza; it is deserted." 27And he rose up and went there. And behold there came a man from Ethiopia, a eunuch, a minister of Candace, the queen of Ethiopia, who was placed in charge of all her treasures. He had come to Jerusalem to worship, 28and was on his way home. He sat in his chariot and was reading the prophet Isaiah.

The conversion of the Ethiopian official is of importance for our picture of the early church. Through him the message of Christ will be carried to the regions of the distant south. Again this is a striking example of the *progress of the word* throughout the world, propagated in every direction and in all quarters. Even the lonely road which ran from Jerusalem to Gaza is traversed. And the one who acts as guide is God himself, his angel, his Spirit.

Who was this man from Ethiopia? He came from that country which is probably somewhere in the region around the Sudan, close to the borders of Upper Egypt in the neighborhood of Aswam. Its inhabitants were Hamites. Queens by the name of Candace ruled the country. It is known that at the time, when Luke wrote the Acts of the Apostles, a lively interest for what was then Ethiopia was shown in the political and cultural circles of Rome. Thus we may assume that Luke deliberately inserted this passage into the Acts of the Apostles for possible Roman readers of his account.

[29]*The Spirit spoke to Philip, " Go and join up with this chariot."* [30]*Philip ran up to it, heard him reading the prophet Isaiah, and asked, " Do you really understand what you are reading?"* [31]*He said, " How can I, if no one interprets it for me?" And he invited Philip to climb up and sit near him.*

This text is filled with important statements. The " Spirit " again guides the steps of the " evangelist," of the person who is commissioned to deliver the message of salvation.

Earlier " the angel of the Lord " was named as the one who had shown Philip the " deserted " desert road between Jerusalem and Gaza (8:26). *Heavenly instructions* whether experienced interiorly or exteriorly, are part and parcel of the vocabulary of the Bible. And within the framework of the New Testament they are characteristic of Lucan writings. We will see them again in the story of the conversion of Saul (9:5–12), in the narrative relating to Cornelius (10:3, 10, and so on), and in the freeing of Peter (12:7ff.); and they are especially intriguing in the way they are introduced into the missionary journeys of Paul (16:7, 8, 9, and so on).

Philip consequently approaches the chariot of the Ethiopian at the bidding of a superior being. The official reads from the Book of Isaiah, the prophet. *He hears him reading aloud. Thus the word of revelation is in a way* a companion for this man. This man is a searcher, a stranger, someone from a far-off country. He comes from the temple. As a pilgrim he wills to subject himself whole-heartedly to the Lord of heaven and earth. Did he acquire the roll of the prophetic text in Jerusalem? And was it his first? No doubt it was one translated into the Greek language, for the translation of the Old Testament in the form of the Septuagint had spread over the world from the birthplace of its translation in Egypt.

The text which Philip overheard was taken from Isaiah 53. We will meet up with it again shortly. Let us examine a few of the implications contained in the speech itself. " Do you really understand what you are reading?" In this question of the " evangelist " there is enunciated a momentous concern of the primitive church. Up to this point we have frequently seen how completely the apostolic proclamation had busied itself extracting from the Old Testament *a newer and more profound meaning*. It sought and found under the cloak of words the revelation of the salvation mystery in Christ Jesus. A text of Paul paraphrases this preoccupation, when in reference to unbelieving Judaism, he states, "For to this day, when the Old Testament is read to them, the selfsame veil remains, for it is not made known to them that the Old Testament is abrogated by Christ. In fact, to this day when Moses is read, a veil is spread over their hearts. But just as soon as they turn again in repentance to the Lord, the veil will be removed" (2 Cor. 3: 14–16; see Ex. 34: 34).

The Ethiopian finds a veil covering the meaning of the Isaian text from which he is reading: "How can I, if no one interprets it for me," he replies to Philip. He expresses both longing and resignation—the characteristics of all searchers. And the Ethiopian asks the man to climb up and stand at his side, a man until then unknown to him. Perhaps he was prompted by some sort of intimation. For how closely this encounter with the truth is bound up with one who had already learned the truth.

[32]*The passage in scripture which he read was this: " He was led like a lamb to slaughter, and as dumb as a lamb before the shearer, and so he did not open his mouth.* [33]*In his humiliation judgment was taken from him; his fate, who will describe it? For his life is taken up from the earth "* (Is. 53: 7f.). [34]*The eunuch turned to Philip and said, " I pray you, about whom does the prophet say this? About himself or about someone else? "* [35]*Philip opened his mouth beginning with this text and announced to him the " good news of Jesus."*

The text is taken from that section of the Book of Isaiah in which in a series of songs *the servant of God* is mentioned expressly. The Septuagint has reproduced, in a free translation rather than in a basically literal rendering, the words of this passage in order to give it a theological turn. It is rather surprising, though, that only this verse is quoted and that subsequent verses, which are much more impressively concerned with the suffering and expiating servant, are omitted. For in those texts which are omitted the prophet foretells of the passion of our Lord: " He bore our griefs; he carried our sorrows; he was wounded for our transgressions. Chastisement for our salvation lay upon him. By his stripes we were healed. All of us like sheep have gone astray, each has gone his own way. And the Lord has laid upon him the iniquity of us all. . . . Nevertheless, he had not done injustice, nor was he deceitful in his mouth " (Is. 53 : 4ff.).

When the official poses the question to which the above text is related, he touches upon a problem which has been hotly debated by Judaism down to the present day. Who is the suffering servant of Isaiah? Jewish theology saw in him—even though not unanimously and with a multiplicity of explanations—a reference to the Messiah who was to come. From her very beginning the church has understood this passage in a messianic sense and has related it to Christ. Even in his sermon on Pentecost (3 : 13), Peter declared that " the God of our fathers glorified his servant, Jesus "—another clear allusion to the prophecy of Isaiah. Philip likewise gave such a meaning to the words of the prophet.

[36]*As they journeyed along the road, they came to some water and the eunuch said, " Look, there is water. What is to prevent me from being baptized? "* [37]*Philip replied, " If you believe from the bottom of your heart, it could be done." He answered, " I believe that Jesus Christ is the Son of God."* [38]*And he ordered the chariot to be stopped, and they both went down into the water, Philip and the official, and he baptized him.* [39]*After they came up out of the water, the Spirit of the Lord carried Philip away and the official saw him no more; he went on his way rejoicing.*

In a few terse sentences the narrative compresses together the meaningful event which ended in the baptism of the Ethiopian, though we are given no details of the primitive Christian catechesis. We could, however, acquire for ourselves some kind of a notion of it, if we should reflect upon the basic statements contained in the mission sermons we have read thus far or pursue attentively those which are still to come, for example " the good news " which Peter announced to Cornelius (Acts 10) or the sermon of Paul in the synagogue of Antioch, in Pisidia (13 : 16ff.).

The Ethiopian is deeply touched by the truth. *His faith impels him to seek the waters of baptism.* Here again Luke makes use of a strikingly symbolic image! On his way through the desert, without forewarning, the pilgrim from Jerusalem is offered that precious element with which, according to the admonition of our Lord, salvation and redemption are coupled. We can feel something of the longing and the joy of the Ethiopian when he cries out, " Look! Here is water! What is to prevent me from being baptized? "

The narrative concludes on a mystifying note. Although the original text is preserved, additions have been made which augment and clarify the original meaning. In harmony with the truly original text, we can hold that Philip really disappeared, as we know such happenings took place in the Old Testament. In the New Testament, this is the sole example of such an incarnational intervention of a superior power. Or we may assume that " the Spirit of the Lord," who in the beginning had guided the footsteps of Philip (8 : 26, 29), now, after completing his task, drives him irresistibly to take up the new task which had been prepared for him. For the meaning of this passage is that the Spirit of God guides his messengers in even the most minute matters.

"He went on his way rejoicing." Did he not have special reason for being joyous? For we know that he was a "eunuch," that he was castrated—and that in accordance with Jewish law, eunuchs were banned from membership in the salvation community. But in the Christian message of salvation there is no such obstacle to acquiring salvation—all that is asked of one is faith.

⁴⁰Philip, however, found himself in Azot and during his wandering through the countryside he proclaimed the good news in all the cities, until he reached Caesarea.

By this sentence, which reminds us of the note appended to 8:25, the story of the seven concludes. Through these two men, Stephen and Philip, an important stage in the development of the church, both inwardly and outwardly, is brought to completion. We can also obtain through them a picture of the activity of the other official auxiliaries of the twelve, whose number must undoubtedly have increased in the interval; and in this way the church herself must have developed.

At the end of the story, in the concluding sentence, we are apprised of the far-reaching activity of Philip. The whole Palestinian coastal area of the Mediterranean is the scene of his apostolic labors. Presumably he preached also in Lydda and Joppe, hence in those cities which Peter would later visit (9:32ff.). When he reached Caesarea is not known. We have already remarked that he might possibly have arrived there only after Peter had finished his remarkable encounter there with Cornelius the centurion. For we are informed that Paul and his companions— Luke among others—went there on their return from his third missionary journey, hence somewhere around the year 58. There

" he entered the house of the evangelist, Philip, who was one of the seven, and stayed there " (21 : 8).

Saul-Paul: His Call and His First Labors (9:1–30)

As we have already stated, we know of the personal bond which tied Luke to Paul. The letters of the Apostle bear witness to this. Specifically, the letters of the captivity, most probably written in Rome, name Luke as Paul's faithful companion (Col. 4:14; Phm. 24), and the second letter to Timothy testifies to this friendship by the touching phrase: " Only Luke is with me " (2 Tim. 4:11). And the so-called " we narratives " of the Acts (16:10ff.; 20:5ff.) show that Luke frequently accompanied Paul on his missionary journeys and was with him at various stages of his imprisonment. We repeat these facts in order to stress the fact that the author of the Acts is bound to Paul by strong personal ties and by special interests. For this reason we can understand why precisely this remarkable narrative of the call of the Apostle is related with such special attention and thoroughness. In three other cases we will meet with a similar preoccupation with details relating to the Apostle of the gentiles.

The Summons of the Lord (9 : 1–9)

THE PERSECUTOR ON HIS WAY (9:1–2)

¹Saul, however, breathing wrath and threats of death against the disciples of the Lord, approached the high priest and ²asked him for letters to the synagogue at Damascus, so that in case he should find followers of this way, be they men or women, he might bring them back as prisoners to Jerusalem.

The name Saul stands ominously at the very beginning of the narrative. We are already acquainted with the bearer of this name through the story of Stephen (7:58; 8:1, 3). Later on it is explained that the name Paul also belonged to this man (13:9). And from that verse onward the Acts uses this form of his name exclusively. Many have pondered over this change of nomenclature. Perhaps it was occasioned and conditioned by the change of sources which the author used, or by the fact that in traveling through non-Jewish mission territory, the Apostle applied this second name to himself, which as a Roman citizen he had a right to since birth. We cannot, therefore, say that at his conversion a Paul was made out of a Saul, as proverbial usage would have us suppose. For even after his baptism the Acts consistently uses the name " Saul " up to 13:9, while in the various letters of the Apostle the name Paul is used exclusively. This custom of using two names is met with frequently in the Judaism of the period, and the New Testament is no exception.

The problem of the interchange of names is not, however, as it might at first appear, a matter of secondary importance, for it contributes to the better understanding of the situation of the early church. Thus when the name Saul is used so emphatically at the beginning of the narrative, this serves to draw the attention of the reader to the fact that the persecution of the Christians, of which mention was made in passing in 8:3, *was still in progress,* and that Saul was beside himself with rage at the Christians. Due to the insertion of the story of Philip, the distress of the Christians was momentarily lost sight of.

We also learn of the fanaticism of Saul on other occasions towards those Jews who turned Christian. In one of his later speeches to the people he confesses, " I persecuted this way unto death, by making prisoners of both men and women and by delivering them to the prisons " (22:4). And in his speech in the presence of Agrippa we read his own words: " Indeed, I had persuaded myself that I must do many mean things in order to express my opposition to the name of Jesus of Nazareth. This I did also in Jerusalem, and I put many of the faithful into prison—for which I had received complete authority from the high priests. And when they were put to death, I cast my vote against them. I tried to compel them to utter blasphemy even by the use of force in all the synagogues and in my boundless rage I persecuted them in foreign cities " (26:9ff.).

Saul was, consequently, extremely active against the church because he had been granted plenipotentiary powers by the supreme ruling body of the Jews. His was not a privately initiated activity, however, but an all-embracing attempt on the part of the Jewish officials *to suppress the rapidly growing Christian community*. Saul was their emissary as well as their instrument. It will not take long before he himself will stand before this same Sanhedrin as prisoner and as defendant for the sake of Christ and personally experience what he himself had at one time inflicted upon the Christians (22:30ff.).

Why did Saul persecute the Christians? Such a question must of necessity be in our minds and move us to pose it. How did he himself answer it? " I am a Pharisee and the son of Pharisees," he cried out during his trial before the assemblage of the Sanhedrin. And in a loud voice he confessed to the enraged people who were taking him prisoner, " I am a Jew, born at Tarsus, in Cilicia, grown to manhood in that city, where I received my education at the feet of Gamaliel in accordance with the rigor of the law; and I was zealous for the things of God, as you all are today " (22:3). In his letter to the Galatians he refers to his " former life in Judaism " and confesses that he formerly " persecuted the church violently." In explanation of this course of action he said that he went " further in my zeal as a Jew than many of my own age and race, so fierce a champion was I of the traditions handed down by my forefathers " (Gal. 1 : 13f.).

He was educated to be a Pharisee, formed interiorly by a passionately guarded traditionalism for the law, moved by the impetuous zeal of the adolescent, glowing with a sense of mission peculiar to Judaism—and he believed that because of a *special religious vocation* he had to wage war against Christianity until he destroyed it, because he conceived it to be a betrayal of Judaism. In his first letter to Timothy, Paul recalls this epic but tragic struggle: " I owe thanks to him who bestowed his strength upon me, Jesus Christ, our Lord, that he judged me worthy and called me to his service, I who had been a blasphemer, a persecutor, and a wretch; but I found mercy, because I did not know what I did in disbelief. The grace of our Lord was vouchsafed to me overflowingly with faith and love in Christ " (1 Tim. 1 : 12ff.).

"Why Do You Persecute Me?" (9:3–9)

³*As he journeyed and neared Damascus, it happened that a light from heaven flashed round about him,* ⁴*and he fell to the ground and heard a voice saying, " Saul, Saul, why do you persecute me?"* ⁵*He replied, " Who are you, Lord?"* ⁶*And the other answered, " I am Jesus, whom you are persecuting. But get up and go into the city, and you will be told what you must do."* ⁷*The men, however, who had accompanied him, stood there speechless; they heard the voice, it is true, but they saw no one.* ⁸*Saul stood up, and although his eyes were open, he was unable*

to see anything. So they took him by the hand and led him into Damascus. ⁹For three days he was unable to see and he ate and drank nothing.

One of the most memorable events in human history is immortalized in this passage. What we do here will be only to attempt to describe what is in itself an indescribable mystery. Of course, the literary freedom and stylistic license which are often found in Luke play some part here, for Luke was not concerned, as we have seen before, with giving an account cluttered with details, but rather with conveying to us the necessary essentials of his story.

This incident on the way to Damascus has been explained in a variety of ways, among them explanations of the event according to purely natural causes or to purely natural associations. Others believe that biological and psychological reasons can explain the religious experience of Saul-Paul. Some experts have even regarded the Apostle's experience as having taken place in the realm of the abnormal and the pathological.

What do we have to say to such explanations? We are faced with an enigmatical reality. In the last instance, theology can only bow its head reverently in the presence of a mystery whose reality has been so *succinctly and emphatically attested to,* that we cannot overlook the probative power of its witness. In addition to the repeated testimony of the Acts, we have clear and unambiguous evidence for what happened at Damascus from the Apostle himself: " Did I not see Jesus, our Lord?" writes Paul in his first letter to the Corinthians (9:1). By these words he clearly recalls his encounter with Jesus on the road to Damascus. And in the same letter we read also: " As the last of these, as one born out of due time, he appeared also to me "

(1 Cor. 15:8)—another recollection of the vision which was accorded to him while he was on his way to Damascus.

It is important that Paul's encounter with the Lord be placed on a par with the appearances of the Risen One to his disciples (see 1 Cor. 15:5ff.). And from all these passages it should be abundantly clear how firmly the apostles themselves were convinced of the genuineness and reality of this personal experience and how they recognized in it the operation of grace conferred upon Saul by the Lord to whom he called out.

Let us pause a moment to meditate upon the episode itself. Damascus hovered within sight. It was about noontime, or at least the other two accounts so inform us (22:6; 26:13). A " light from heaven suddenly shone round about him." " More brilliant than the rays of the sun " is the description offered in 26:13. Even his companions were affected by it, for " all fell to the ground " (26:14). What kind of a light was it? Have we the right to ask such a question? We know from the gospels how the intervention of heavenly power is very frequently accompanied by a *mysterious light*. The Shepherds in the fields near Bethlehem were bathed in the glory of God (Lk. 2:9); at the Transfiguration of Jesus (Lk. 9:29), the angel of the resurrection appeared and the persons in the scene were irradiated by the glow of light. All these occasions attest to the presence of heavenly illumination; and in the Acts of the Apostles we read that when Peter was freed from prison, " an angel of the Lord entered, and light shone into the room " (12:7). This light is a symbol, a reflection of that light which in the language of the Bible is like the inscrutable glory of God.

A voice addresses the man prone on the ground: " Saul, Saul, why do you persecute me?" These words are also to be found in parallel passages; and in verse 26:14 it is noted expressly that the voice made use of the Hebrew tongue. We can draw this conclusion from the name Saul, by which he was addressed. The self-revealing Lord spoke to him in his *mother tongue,* which was essentially more familiar to Paul than Greek, although he was Hellenic in origin. Or is it simply a sign that the Transfigured Christ wished to speak to him in that language which he himself had used while here upon earth? Did he wish to call Saul to serve him in the apostleship in the same tongue with which he had summoned the twelve?

For it is Jesus who speaks in this way, Jesus the Risen and Transfigured One. And we take for granted that Saul saw *the person of Jesus.* In his speech before Agrippa it is reported that the message of Jesus to Paul was simply: " I have appeared to you that I might appoint you to be a servant and a witness of that which you saw in me, and of that in which I would show myself to you " (26:16). And in the same speech Paul mentions the heavenly appearance towards whom he reacted not as one rejecting a proposal (26:19). " Did I not see the Lord?" the Apostle wrote to the Corinthians, with his thoughts focussed on the event at Damascus (1 Cor. 9:1). It was consequently a face-to-face encounter which Saul experienced, one which was vouchsafed only to him and not to his companions. These companions saw no one, even though they were surrounded by an inexplicable light (26:13). It is not our task to explain further what happened at that moment. Rather we must confess that we can only accept and reverently meditate upon what the narrative permits us to recognize and to learn.

" Who are you, Lord?" Saul retorts. In all three narratives of the conversion, a question followed by another question in answer to the first is the way in which the conversation is carried out. Were the words imprinted so deeply on the heart of the

Apostle that he was never able to forget them? It would be only natural to assume this, for they were of such decisive importance. What kind of information was Saul trying to acquire by answering one question with another? Did he recognize Jesus immediately? Or did he frame his query as he did because he was unacquainted with the Unknown One? We do not know for certain whether earlier he had personally made the acquaintance of Jesus.

Henceforth Jesus will place his hand upon his shoulder and take possession of him. *As servant of Christ Jesus,* as he calls himself in his letter, he now belongs to his *Kyrios,* his Lord, for whom he was called. From now on his life will be one of unique obedience. He who had traveled to Damascus, armed with the warrants of the high priest, to bring back to Jerusalem the disciples of Jesus, is himself seized by the superior power of God and proceeds, led by his companions, as a prisoner of Christ, to the city he had sought out in order to follow out the directions of the voice : " Get up, go into the city, and you will be told what you must do." This compliance is even more sharply stressed in the clauses of what is known as " the original or essential " text, where we read, " Trembling and stuttering, he said : ' Lord, what will you have me do? ' "

Conversion and Baptism (9 : 10–22)

COMMISSION GIVEN TO ANANIAS (9:10–12)

[10]*At Damascus there was a disciple by the name of Ananias, and Jesus spoke to him in a vision: " Ananias." He answered, " I am here, Lord." *[11]*The Lord said to him, " Get up and go into*

*the street called Straight and in the house of Judas inquire about
a man from Tarsus by the name of Saul. For behold, he prays."*
[12]*And he saw in a vision a man, named Ananias, enter and lay
his hands upon him, that he might see again.*

Again the text is of importance for an understanding of the
church. The mystery behind the action of grace is made visual
and graphic. As it was the Transfigured Christ himself who had
initiated the work of conversion, so now he entrusts its completion to the church. Does he in this instance wish to make clear
how important the *mediatorship* of the purely human is in the
work of salvation, deputed now to the church? This man Ananias
from Damascus was the mediator for Saul but only in so far as
his insertion into the community of the church was concerned—
an insertion which was to be accomplished through baptism and
the laying-on of hands.

In our narrative the event is divided into various segments,
scenes in which the whole is revealed. *Precise instructions* are
given to Ananias. He appears to have lived in Damascus for quite
some time. The same may be said of the unknown Judas who
dwelt on the street called " Straight." We do not possess any other
details, though we are made conscious of the fact that divine
instructions are given down to the minutest detail, so that the
work of conversion and vocation may be completed according to
God's plan. For the first time we are supplied with data concerning Saul, when he is characterized as " a man from Tarsus."
Later on, this circumstance will be corroborated. Was Tarsus
more definitive for Saul than Jerusalem, from which he had set
out on his journey to Damascus? Without doubt, something
significant for the person and for the labors of Paul the apostle
is concealed in the fact that he traced his origin to Tarsus.

" For behold, he is praying." What is meant by this incidental remark? The phrase affords us a discreet glance at the spiritual life of a man seized by divine grace. Without eating or drinking (9:9), without being able to see anything with the naked eye, he devotes himself to three days of solitude in the darkness of blindness to ready himself for whatever the Lord has prepared for him. This is a truly impressive picture. He *prays*. As a Jew he had also prayed. As a persecutor of the Christians he certainly prayed to God. What was the content of his prayers? We confess our ignorance. But we may venture a conjecture that it contributed to his interior growth, for the person whom he had glimpsed, bathed in light, must have impressed himself so deeply on his soul that he could only stutter and plead that God be merciful to him. And what we cannot forget is how often and how urgently this same man will later on speak of the power and the necessity of prayer in his own letters.

Paul did not spend these three days in utter darkness without consolation of any sort. The blind man was accorded *a vision*. " And he saw in a vision a man, named Ananias, enter and lay his hands upon him that he might see again." The sentence in which this fact is enunciated occupies a peculiar place in the text. It is not readily apparent whether or not it is part of the speech of our Lord to Ananias or whether it is an independent statement supplementing the remarks of the author. Both are possibilities. If we could see in these words part of the message delivered by the voice of God, we could conceive that through them Ananias was being encouraged to carry out a task which to him appeared otherwise so incomprehensible and dangerous, because Saul would in fact be prepared for his coming by the vision which had been granted him. But if this is a note of the author —and this appears to us to be more likely—then it could possibly mean that at the moment Ananias was being commissioned by the Lord, Saul was being consoled by the vision which was intended to prepare him for his visitant.

THE PURPOSE OF THE MISSION (9:13-16)

[13]Ananias replied, " Lord, I have heard from many about this man, what evil he has wreaked on the saints in Jerusalem. [14]And even here he possesses warrants granted him by the high priests, to put irons on everyone who calls upon your name." [15]The Lord, however, said to him, " Go there. He is my chosen instrument to carry my name before the peoples and to the kings and the sons of Israel. [16]For I will show him what he must suffer for my name's sake."

Ananias experiences shock at the news of the task which is being thrust upon him. By his objection, the work of grace—which had to be perfected according to God's decree—appears now in all its clarity for the first time. What appears unthinkable and impossible to human reason can be brought to pass by the freely granted love and the benign providence of God. The Apostle is chosen without merit of any kind, in fact without a hint at anything which could remind us of merit. Yet anyone who is caught up in the magnanimity of divine grace is called by and likewise enabled to preach the salvific will of God purely and convincingly—as we learn from Paul's letters.

The reputation which Saul had acquired preceded him to Damascus and caused the Christians there to tremble in fear. We are made cognizant of this in the words of Ananias. The disciples of Jesus are called " saints." In 9:32 we also hear of the "saints in Lydia." Frequently we read of the same genre of people in the letters of the Apostle. For the essence of being a Christian is captured in this word. This quality of holiness in the Christian is based on the mystery of Jesus and also on being baptized in his name, in whom we profess our faith while receiving the sacrament. "Those who call upon your name" is the way in which Ananias singles out the "saints"; and by this statement we are reminded of the words of Joel included in the pentecostal sermon of Peter: "Everyone who invokes the name of the Lord will be saved" (2:21).

Ananias appreciates the nobility of being a Christian, of the mystery with which the saints are filled to overflowing. He knows of Saul, the arch-enemy of the church. How should he interpret the directions which are now given him? An unprecedented agitation stirs in the depth of his soul, a tension between human calculation and *the unfathomable undecipherability of divine activity*. It will always be normal for us to think and to act as Ananias did. With how much difficulty do we arrive at what Paul—certainly fully aware of the personal guidance he was receiving—tries to express in his letter to the Romans: "Oh, the depth of the riches, of the wisdom, and of the knowledge of God. How unfathomable are his judgments and how unsearchable his ways! For who has known the mind of the Lord? Or who has been his counsellor? Or who has given him a gift, whereby he might be repaid?" (Rom. 11:33ff.).

The Lord gives Ananias his instructions. Rarely is such exciting information imparted to man. "He is the chosen instrument of mine." Is this the same Saul, then, who came to Damascus "breathing wrath and threats against the disciples of the Lord"? *What is so peculiar about God's choice?* We must remain silent in the face of the freedom and the uniqueness of God! "O man, who are you to answer back to God?" Paul will later on write time and again to the Romans (9:20). And in his letters he will recurrently recall the election which he perceived in himself. His message of grace is more than a theological theory, for he has personally experienced it.

Saul will be "a chosen instrument." In his Epistle to the Galatians he gives voice to this idea: "When it pleased him to reveal his Son in one who had been set aside from the womb of his mother onward, so that I might proclaim him among the gentiles . . ." He was chosen not because of his own personal talents, but because of the business of salvation. He must be *an ambassador* for the "Lord." He must become a witness in the same way as the others were and bear testimony as they did. And he was being readied for this by being commissioned as were the twelve. His task as well as theirs was that of proclaiming the Risen One (1:8). "People and kings" were to form his audiences; before them he will preach. The whole non-Jewish world is comprised under these terms; and the Acts of the Apostles will shortly describe it. The "sons of Israel" will also listen to the "good tidings," as Luke will later declare. "He will carry my name" before all of them: this means that he will proclaim the message of Jesus Christ, which is a message of salvation for all people without distinction of race, color, or former religion.

A seldom employed, a rare phrase is added to the message of the Lord to Ananias: "For I will show him what he must suffer for my name's sake." *To suffer for the sake of Christ:* this will be the portion of the Apostle from the hour before Damascus onward. This the Acts of the Apostles will bear witness to; this Paul's letters will attest to in truly stirring fashion. This is a unique law of discipleship in Christ, so contrary to sheer human sensibility. Christ himself underwent the sufferings of his passion. For he had to, as we are informed so bluntly in the gospel: " Did not Christ have to suffer this in order to enter into his glory?" Thus the Risen One inquires of the two disciples on the way to Emmaus.

THE CURE AND THE BAPTISM (9:17–19a)

17*Then Ananias went to him, entered into the house, laid his hands on him, and said, " Brother Saul, the Lord Jesus who appeared to you along the way by which you came has sent me, so that you may see again and be filled with the Holy Spirit."* 18*Immediately there fell scales as it were from his eyes and he was able to see again. He stood up and was baptized,* 19a*and he took food and regained his strength.*

Ananias fulfilled the instructions which were given him by the Lord. He did what he was supposed to do—so we may be permitted to suppose with wonderment at the ways of God and grace. Saul was forced to wait for him three days (9:9). What could have passed through his mind during that length of time? He was incapable of seeing anything, and he refused both food and drink. These days were, however, filled out by *an interior illumination*. " Look, he prays," our Lord says to Ananias. And the hint in verse 12 permits us to surmise that even though in darkness the days did not pass without any consolation being afforded the blind man. The vision had assured Saul that one would come who would open the eyes shuttered to light.

" Brother Saul ": with such a familiar, friendly phrase Ananias greets this persecutor of the Christians who up to that moment had been so feared by the community. He employed the Hebrew form of the name, that form with which Saul had heard himself addressed by the Lord before Damascus. Advisedly Ananias reminds him of the Lord who had appeared to him on the way. All this was a sign to Saul that the one who now stood in his presence was indeed one who had been sent by the Lord. By reason of his task of mediator this man was singled out to bring him both a cure for his physical blindness and the indwelling of the Holy Spirit for his soul—as gifts of the Lord. And " he was able to see again." Was the blindness of Saul genuine? Without doubt—even though we are unable to offer any kind of scientific medical explanation for it. It was also, however, a symbol, a symbol of the night that had enveloped him thus far and a symbol for the way in which he had previously acted. He is now permitted to gaze at *a new light*. And this is a parable. To the physical eyesight which is restored to him is added an enlightenment of the spirit, an insight into the mystery of Jesus. We think here chiefly of that renowned passage in the second letter to the Corinthians: " All of us, when we reflect with unveiled countenance the glory of God, are changed into his likeness, from glory to glory, as this radiates from the Spirit of the Lord " (2 Cor. 3 : 18).

" He could see again, and stood up and was baptized." This was the baptism of Saul-Paul. It was a baptism in the name of him whom three days before he had persecuted with such " wrath and threats of death." And in his confession of faith at his baptism he cries out the name against which, as he testifies before Agrippa, he had felt he would have to undertake such horrendous persecution. He rose up from out of the water a new man. " He ate some food and regained his strength." This holds true not only for his body. It also holds true of the power of the

Spirit, for it was the Holy Spirit who held such a grip on him that he would never again be able to break loose from it.

His First Labors and Sufferings (9 : 19b–30)

SERMON IN DAMASCUS (9:19b–22)

[19b]*He remained several days with the disciples at Damascus,* [20]*and in all the synagogues without delay he testified that Jesus was the Son of God.* [21]*All who heard him were amazed and remarked, " Is not this the man who sought to root up in Jerusalem all those who called on this name? And he came here with the express purpose of taking them prisoners and then taking them bound back to the high priests."* [22]*Saul, however, became more confident day by day and confounded the Jews living in Damascus by demonstrating that this man was the Messiah.*

The genuine Paul now stands before us. We recognize him from his letters as he now is: a person of perfervid activity, animated by an ardent will to accomplish what he recognized to be his duty. Just as any other persecutor he had stalked his prey; but now he increasingly busies himself with the task of proclaiming Christ. Yet anyone who compares the chronological data of the letter to the Galatians with that contained in this passage will be faced with certain difficulties, if he should try to bring them into harmony. In that letter we learn that he " did not turn to flesh and blood and did not go up to Jerusalem like those who were apostles before him, but I went away to Arabia; and then I returned again to Damascus " (Gal. 1 : 16f.).

Yet it is not so difficult to reconcile this discrepancy as one might suppose. For when, as the letter states, Paul returned from

Arabia to Damascus, he did not want to create the impression that he had been there before he went to Arabia, precisely in connection with his call. Luke merely neglected to mention his stay in Arabia because in presenting his picture of Paul he wanted to be as concise as possible; certainly he does not want to exclude such a sojourn. Here he is far more concerned with showing how from being a persecutor Saul forthwith becomes a witness, a bearer of " good news "; he is a persecutor transformed into a witness. Even in Arabia, which lies in the territory to the east of Damascus, he had been active as a messenger of the faith. And he did this, as even our narrative appears to express it, because he was conscious of the fact that he had been directly chosen by our Lord for his service.

We can understand the *confusion and the consternation* which Saul's stay in Damascus must have caused. The people knew that he had come, armed with warrants from the high priests. He wanted to take prisoners all those " who invoked this name." And now of all places he appears in the synagogue and gives testimony to that very name. " Jesus, the Son of God!" " Jesus, the Messiah!" With that name on his lips he calls out to the horrified Jews who formed his audience. Enraged by what they heard, the Jews rose up and sought to counter the danger which now beset them. Nor was this the last time that Jews would demonstrate to the Apostle what he would have to suffer for the name of Christ (9:16).

FLIGHT FROM DAMASCUS (9: 23–25)

[23]*After a number of days had passed, the Jews formulated a plan to kill him.* [24]*Saul, however, learned of their scheme. Day and night they watched the gates to rid themselves of him.* [25]*But the*

disciples took him and by night got him over the wall, by letting him down in a basket.

We are still within the Judeo-Christian epoch of the church. Everything which the apostles experienced, namely, opposition and violence, were leveled against them by the Jews. Saul knew these things all too well. Now he had to endure *in his own person* " how much evil " he had previously inflicted upon the saints (9 : 13). The same fate which Stephen suffered threatened to engulf him. The one who had guarded the clothing of those who stoned Stephen seems to be in line himself to become a sacrificial victim. How frequently in relating the labors of the Apostle the Acts is compelled to narrate similar situations in which he now found himself. But ever and again it will be true what the Lord had said to Paul on the road to Damascus : " I will deliver you from the people and from the gentiles, to whom I send you " (26 : 17).

" Saul learned of their scheme." The " disciples," that is, the Jewish Christians of Damascus, took upon themselves the task of protecting him—the very same people whom he had come to Damascus to arrest. Now it should have been astonishingly clear to the former persecutor how pitifully all human beginnings must grind to a stop when they are pitted against the counsels of God. In the darkness of the night as the basket scrapes against the wall of the city of Damascus, Saul cowers within it. Agitated, necessarily both internally and externally, he enters upon his return journey, deprived of all human protection, but delivered over to the grace of God, who called him and in whom from now he will place his full trust. " My grace is sufficient for you," the Lord assures him later on, " for strength is perfected in infirmity."

That we are not dealing in this flight over the wall with an excerpt from some pious legend, contrived to arouse our sympathy, but with authentic history, is attested to in the same letter to the Corinthians when in remembrance of that flight Paul tells us, " At Damascus the governor of King Aretas ordered the city to be put under guard with the intention of seizing me, but through a window I was let down the wall in a basket and thus escaped his hands " (2 Cor. 11 : 32f.). This sentence is to be found alongside the passage, " And if I must boast, I will boast of my weakness. God, the father of our Lord, Jesus Christ, he who is blessed for all eternity, knows that I do not lie " (2 Cor. 11 : 30f.).

ENCOUNTER WITH THE MOTHER COMMUNITY (9: 26–30)

[26]*When he reached Jerusalem, he tried to join the disciples; but they all feared him, since they did not believe that he was a disciple.* [27]*Barnabas, however, befriended him, brought him to the apostles, and told them how on the road he had seen the Lord and that the Lord had spoken to him, and how in Damascus he had courageously preached the name of Jesus.* [28]*And so he moved in and out among them in Jerusalem and taught boldly in the name of the Lord.* [29]*He spoke also to the Hellenists and held discussions with them. These, however, tried to rid themselves of him.* [30]*When the brothers heard of this, they took him down to Caesarea and sent him off to Tarsus.*

Several motives may have caused Saul to turn his footsteps towards Jerusalem after fleeing from Damascus. The most decisive was, no doubt, to get into contact with the mother community and with its leaders, the apostles. He certainly did what he did at great personal risk, because he was that person whom the Jews in Damascus had tried to murder; now he permits himself to be seen in Jerusalem. He appreciated the dangers which beset him on both sides: on the part of the Christians—for he had so passionately sought to destroy them by his persecutions; and on the part of the Jews—logically they would treat him as a traitor and turncoat. In spite of everything he nevertheless chose Jerusalem as the base of his operations. He did what he did with full consciousness of his mission. The summons of God still rings in his ears. In spite of his knowledge of the immediacy of his vocation, he did not overlook *his necessary submission to the community of the church*. Paul was indeed of a temperament characterized by evident self-willfulness and also by a sense of personal responsibility; at the same time, however, he recognized the profound significance and the undeniable claim of the church founded by Christ and he submitted to her authority.

Let us avoid any possible exegetical explanation of the problem —which is also connected with Paul's further visits to Jerusalem —and concentrate on one fact which is irrefutable and univocal, namely, that this former enemy and opponent of the church devotes his efforts towards *establishing contact with the leadership of the church*, towards more meaningful contacts with his confreres. He does this not as a mere disciple of Christ, but as one commissioned, as an ambassador of the Lord, in whose service he has already labored for three years. For we take for granted that his stay in Arabia, mentioned in the letter to the Galatians, served the work of proclamation as did his days in Damascus. By such an explanation, the theory that Paul sought out the solitude of Arabia simply to prepare himself seriously for his task of spreading the gospel cannot be labeled as meaningless. For we cannot imagine how a man with the temperament of Paul could spend so much time indulging himself, as it were, solely in meditation. In fact, the letter to the Galatians assumes that the man called to be an apostle immediately applied himself to the task implied in his vocation, for we read for the period covered by the first three years: " To the Christian communities of Judea I was not known by sight: ' He who once persecuted us now proclaims the faith which he once sought to blot out ' " (Gal. 1 : 22f.).

Our text tells us that during the first visit in Jerusalem he was chiefly concerned about the apostles: " Barnabas, however, befriended him, brought him to the apostles, and told how on the road he had seen the Lord and that the Lord had spoken to him, and how in Damascus he had courageously preached the name of Jesus." And if we should further take for granted from the data supplied us in the letter to the Galatians, that he was anxious " to seek out Cephas," we would perceive how this man sought *to obtain a place for himself in the visible structure of the church,* this man in whose original disposition can be found strong tendencies to independence and self-decision and who risked to a certain extent his finding of the road to Christ in solitude. And when in his letters he stresses in a special way the name of Cephas, that is, Peter, then we dare not overlook the fact that he was aware of Peter's special position in the church and that he wished to give him the respect which he deserved. And although in this same letter to the Galatians we are informed of a memorable and untoward incident in Antioch, in which Paul turned defiantly and openly against Peter and took him to task for his manner of acting (Gal. 2 : 11f.), we should not see in it anything derogating from or in contradiction to his recognition of Peter's authority. We recognize in all this with what frankness and candor the men of the church behave towards one another, free of solemn aloofness or courtly toadying.

It is *Barnabas* who takes the part of the newcomer from Damascus. Somewhat earlier we made the acquaintance of this awesome personage (4 : 36). He is one of the most prepossessing personalities to be found in the early church. We have also said that we may without cavil think that Luke held him in great respect, and he soon became a good friend of Paul. In him we recognize how important the relation of person-to-person is prized by God for the fulfillment of his plans. " What would Paul have been without Barnabas?" we would like to ask, especially when later on we shall see how it is Barnabas who will summon Paul, all but forgotten, to join him in a common enterprise in Antioch (11 : 25f.), and will win him over to undertake his first great missionary journey (13 : 2ff.). It will certainly be painful for both these long-time friends, when at the outset of the second great missionary journey they failed to see eye-to-eye about taking John Marcus, the cousin of Barnabas, along with them, and so for a time they went their separate ways.

Paul was unable to enjoy for any length of time his association with the mother church. The circumstances were tense; his temperament was hasty and stormy. He believed that his former friends, the Hellenic Jews, had to be won over to the message that he preached. These were the same ones who could not stomach Stephen. They *threatened him, Paul, with a like fate.* But the " brothers," the Christians and especially the apostles among them, took precautions to ensure the safety of Paul. They conducted him to the seaport of Caesarea, and from there sent him on his way to Tarsus, to his home-city. Again he embarks on flight. Again those who save him are the very ones to whom he had threatened death and destruction a short time before.

Again he learns what the Lord meant when he said to Ananias, " I will show him how much he must suffer for the sake of my name."

The Labors of Peter (9:31—11:18)

In Lydda and Joppe (9: 31-43)

A LOOK AT THE CHURCH (9: 31)

³¹*The church enjoyed peace in the whole of Judea, Galilee, and Samaria. She built herself up, walked in fear of the Lord, and increased in numbers under the guidance of the Holy Spirit.*

Paul withdrew from the territory of Palestine, in which he had caused so much unrest. " Then I went into the regions of Syria and Cilicia " (Gal. 1:21), without giving a reason for his hasty departure from Jerusalem. We know nothing of how he spent the subsequent years. It is no doubt a period of peace for the man who had been so affected by the unrest he had personally stirred up. And the land of Judea was also at peace. *Peace* settled down even over the church. The three territories of Palestine are named for good reason. We observe with special attention how the word " church " in this passage means the church universal, whereas in other pericopes in the Acts of the Apostles the same title is meant to designate individual churches.

As Luke is accustomed to doing in presenting his materials, he first offers us an over-all, comprehensive view of the state of the church, before he proceeds to furnish us with individual details of her history. " She built herself up." The strengthening and the deepening of the exterior life of the growing community follow closely upon its outward spread. We are still, however, dealing with the beginnings of the church, in that period in which she still busied herself with her mission to Judaism. But her development itself becomes so rapid that the apostolic proclamation of the " good news " deliberately oversteps its self-imposed boundaries and forges ahead into the domain of the non-Jewish world. As we shall soon see, it will be Peter himself to whom as the chief representative of the universal church the way will be shown and opened for the start of the missions to the gentiles. In the many endeavors which the Acts of the Apostles narrates, always the Holy Spirit fills the church and guides her faltering steps. Even the abbreviated excerpt which we have quoted above inculcates this lesson, when in its conclusion we read: " And the church increased in numbers under the guidance of the Holy Spirit."

The Healing of the Sick in Lydda (9:32–35)

[32]Then it happened that on his way through the countryside Peter came to the holy ones who lived in Lydda. [33]There he met a man with the name of Aeneas who had been bedridden for eight years; he was a paralytic. [34]Peter said to him, "Aeneas, Jesus Christ gives you back your health. Arise and make your own bed!" And immediately he stood up. [35]All who lived in Lydda and in the neighborhood of Saron saw him and were converted to the Lord.

Three very important stories about Peter follow one another in rapid succession; and a very definite climactic arrangement can

be discerned both in regard to content and to size. Thus we may
—in accordance with Luke's method of presentation—see in
them certain similarities which remind us of similar incidents in
the public life of Jesus and likewise in kindred narratives in
Paul. Yet, despite all literary kinship, each story possesses its
own unique identity and each depicts graphically the image and
the course of the church's development. We are again made
cognizant of the fact that in the person of Peter resides the
authority of the community in Jerusalem, whose reputation rests
on the apostles.

The apostle no doubt visited more than only Lydda, though
the text offers no particulars as to the exact reason for the journey
itself. But if we are permitted to assume that on this occasion
also (as in 8:14) he was sent by the apostolic college, this would
in no way derogate from either the unique authority or the
unique position which the apostles clearly accorded him. We
may also observe that on this trip he journeyed alone—without
the companionship of John.

We may compare in detail the healing of the paralytic, Aeneas,
with the miracle of the man born lame at the " beautiful gate "
(3:1). Both narratives agree in most particulars. But in this
comparison we cannot afford to overlook certain important discrepancies. These are evident in the words which are used to
address the sick man. At the healing of the man born lame,
Peter said, " In the name of Jesus Christ of Nazareth, rise and
go from here "; in this latter incident the words by which the
cure was affected are as follows: " Aeneas, Jesus Christ gives
you back your health." The human person is relegated more
thoroughly to the background in contrast to the *power of healing which Jesus Christ had bestowed upon the apostle.* Again
the miracle is presented as a familiar sign of the witness to the

proclamation of the " good news " in Christ. In this story its listeners are brought to realize the presence of a higher Power; they become conscious of the truth of the word which the apostles preach to them.

THE RAISING OF THE DEAD IN JOPPE (9:36–43)

As a narrative dealing with Peter, this story is located within its own definite literary framework. Peter's position, his reputation, and his gift of healing become more evident here than in the previous cure of the paralytic Aeneas. The raising of a person from the dead cannot—as would be possible in a cure of a sick person—be explained away on the assumption that it is merely an exercise in the power of suggestion. Such a prodigy lies far beyond the realm of human power. Peter also realized this. His conduct reminds us of that of the prophet Elijah, who carried the dead son of the widow of Sareptha to an upper room and praying over him restored him to life (1 Kgs. 17:17ff.). A similar case is also recounted of Eliseus (2 Kgs. 4:32ff.). We cannot deny that in its outward form this story has a certain kinship with both these Old Testament narratives. But this fact does not permit us to question the genuineness of Peter's miracles, although it is possible that the incident receives the form it does because the author recalled some Old Testament narratives or other tales of miracles.

[36]*Now in Joppe there was a disciple by the name of Tabitha— translated her name means Dorcas or Gazelle. She abounded in good works and alms which she distributed prodigally. *[37]*But it happened at this time that she became ill and died. After they had washed her, they laid her out in an upper room. *[38]*Since Lydda lies close to Joppe, the disciples heard that Peter was staying there, and so they sent two men to him with the plea, " Come to us here without delay." *[39]*Peter arose and went with them. When he arrived, they led him up to the upper room;*

*and all the widows came to meet him; with tears in their eyes
they showed him the coats and the garments which Dorcas had
made for them while she was still among them.* ⁴⁰*Then Peter
ordered them all out of the room, knelt down, prayed, and turning to the corpse, said, " Tabitha, arise!"* ⁴¹*He gave her his hand
and lifted her up. Then he summoned the saints and the widows
and presented her to them alive.* ⁴²*This became known all over
Joppe, and many believed in the Lord.* ⁴³*As befitted the occasion,
he stopped for a while at Joppe with a certain Simon, a tanner.*

Peter knew that he had been graced by a charism, because he
could never have accomplished what he did by his own native
talents, with his own unaided human powers. He did, however,
believe in the *omnipotence of God.* And so falling to his knees
and praying, he begged the miracle from him. With a keen
awareness of the active presence of God he was able to say:
" Tabitha, arise!" Here again we are confronted with our inability to explain the incident. We are again in the presence of
a mystery of God's providence. Not without reason does the
" Western text " make an addition to the words of Peter, con-
joining to them the following phrase: " Rise, in the name of the
Lord Jesus!" We are again in the presence of a mystery. The
Lord makes known his presence in the church. We are reminded
here of that passage in which in his farewell address to his
apostles Jesus states, " Truly, truly, I say to you: he who believes
in me will perform the same works which I do and he will
perform even greater ones than these; because I go to the Father,
and whatever you shall ask for in my name that I will do, so that
the Father may be glorified in his Son " (Jn. 14:12ff.). Only by
such a revelation can we accept in deep faith the genuineness of
the miracle-event such as is described here.

Tabitha is presented to us as one of the *noblest women of the infant church*. " She abounded in good works and in alms which she distributed prodigally." The " coats " and " garments " which she made for the poor demonstrate to us that she was one of those rare women who are able to unite in a truly spiritual fashion piety and a practical sense of charity towards others. It does not alter matters the least whether we consider her to be an officially recognized " deaconess," as for example Phoebe, the deaconess of the community of Cenchreae (Rom. 16: 1), or whether we hold that she performed her works of charity entirely on her own initiative. We know from the various books of the New Testament how intimately the image of the collaborating, empathetic woman is linked up with the growth of the church; it is one and the same whether we recall the pious group who collected around Jesus, as this is so charmingly sketched for us by Luke (8: 2), or whether we think of the women who are mentioned in the Acts of the Apostles and in the letters of Paul. We need only consider chapter 16 of the Epistle to the Romans where within short compass we find enumerated the names of Phoebe, Prisca, Maria, Tryphaena; Tryphosa, Persis, and Julia, in order to realize with what gratitude Paul recalls these women in order to keep fresh the memory of their example and of their service in the work of proclaiming the message of salvation.

When at the conclusion of the story, it is stated that Peter stayed for a while in Joppe with a certain *Simon, a tanner,* this is written expressly because of its relevance to the subsequent narrative (10: 16). At the same time, the success which attended the labors of the apostle in Joppe is carefully pointed out. This is again self-evident proof of the importance of a miracle as witness to the " good news." When the author makes express mention of the trade plied by the host, he may have done so for a special reason. We know that the trade of a tanner was looked upon as unclean and not held in high esteem by the teachers of the law and the Scribes. Peter's taking up quarters at the home of a tanner may be construed as a sign that he felt himself to be free of any and all Pharisaical prejudices and that he wished to give us an insight into himself as he prepares for the important instruction which he will receive in the following narrative.

Conversion of the Centurion Cornelius (*10:1–11:18*)

With chapter 10 we reach the climax in the story of the progress of the early church. The external bulk of the story alone permits us to draw such a conclusion. To this we may add the fact that in verses 11:1–18 the externals are again augmented by a plethora of details in the form of a personal narrative offered by Peter. Peter himself is again the principal figure. We have the impression that these three narratives, namely, from 9:31—11:8, centering as they do on Peter, had originally formed a part of a continuous tradition and as such were absorbed by Luke into his own narrative. They are geographically closely intertwined; from Lydda Peter is called to Joppe, from Joppe he eventually goes to Caesarea. All three cities are adjacent to one another along the coastline.

The *uniqueness of this story* lies in the fact that through Peter the Christian community comes for the first time into contact with a non-Jew, and thus a gentile is received into the church. How important and how portentous this was for the growth of the church is demonstrated at the so-called Council of the Apostles. In this gathering the fundamental and practical regulations concerning the mission of the church to the gentile world and concerning the recognition of the proclamation of the faith, free of all restrictions imposed by the law as advocated by Paul, are formulated and promulgated for all. During the course of an extremely heated debate, Peter arose and said, "Brothers, you know that from the very first days God made his choice known to you, that by my mouth the gentiles should receive the word of the gospel and profess their faith " (15:7f.).

Actually we are dealing here with the *inauguration of an important decision* which will affect the entire course of the church's preaching effort. Up to this point in the narrative, the apostles' activities were directed exclusively to the Jews. This does not mean that they had only a Judeo-Christian church in mind. We should not interpret the important commission given by the Risen One and his commission to convert the whole world as anything but genuine and authentic. But before that commission could be put into practice, the message of salvation was to be preached first of all to that people to whom, by the mysterious providence of God, there had been entrusted a special revealed covenant which was to last for thousands of years. The mission to make disciples of the " whole world " was surely present in the consciousness of the apostles from the very beginning, but a great many obstacles were placed in the way of its realization. These were to be found chiefly in the unsurmountable barriers which Judaism had by reason of her long educative process raised between herself and the non-Judaic world. Exercising an especially great influence over Jews wishing to become Christians were the so-called ceremonial laws, whose vocabulary was filled with such terms as " clean " and " unclean "—so many, in fact, that in the beginning the apostles themselves were beset by the great difficulty of uprooting such deeply enrooted convictions. To these ceremonial requirements we must add the Jewish concept of circumcision, to which the people ascribed such salvific significance that a Jew could scarcely conceive it possible that without its taking place the way to salvation was open. God himself in his admonition to Peter had to intervene to show the church how to remove the shackles and to dissipate the solidified notions of cleanness and uncleanness. Thus the road shown to Peter by which he was to proceed from Caesarea to Cornelius was as decisive and important as was the call of Saul before Damascus.

We conclude from the fullness of detail and from the forcefulness with which the reception of Cornelius into the church is described that this was the *first decision made in this matter* in the early church. By saying this, however, we touch upon another question: How is this story related to the baptism of the Ethiopian official narrated in chapter 8? In our review of that story we briefly formulated the query without being able to answer it with any degree of certainty. No doubt the conversion of the Ethiopian offered no problem. If the eunuch were the first gentile to have been baptized, however, perhaps Philip would have deliberated with himself more thoroughly or he would have sought help, as was done in the case of Cornelius with so much detail. We therefore must leave the question open whether or not the eunuch was indeed a gentile.

We are now led to another special reason which makes the conversion of Cornelius so interesting and of such importance for the Acts of the Apostles. What is this reason? Cornelius is a Roman officer, as this is made abundantly clear to us in 10:24 and 10:44. We assume for weighty reasons that he was also a member of a famous Roman family of the same name. We know, now, how carefully the Acts were written with an eye to Rome and with special consideration for a Roman readership. Thus the story of Cornelius was a God-given opportunity for Luke to relate to the gentiles a precedent which must have been of supreme importance.

The Message of the Centurion (10:1–8)

¹*A man in Caesarea, by the name of Cornelius, the centurion of the so-called Italian cohort, ²pious and God-fearing, who together with his family and household distributed alms so generously to the people and prayed to God without ceasing, ³saw clearly in a vision, at about the ninth hour of the day, an angel of God approaching him; the angel said, " Cornelius!" ⁴He gazed at him, and, seized with fright, said, " What is it, Lord?" The angel replied, " Your prayers and your alms have ascended as a memorial before God. ⁵Send some men to Joppe and let them*

bring here a certain Simon, with the surname Peter; ⁶he is lodging with Simon, the tanner, whose house is on the seashore; he will tell you what you must do." ⁷When the angel who had spoken to him disappeared, he summoned two of his servants and a God-fearing soldier of the cohort subject to him, ⁸explained to them everything that had happened, and sent them to Joppe.

In these few lines Luke gives us a graphic picture of a nobleman as well as an officer. We are cognizant of the attention with which on other occasions Luke delineates high-ranking officials, especially of the Roman army and government. Thus we are reminded of the centurion at Capharnaum upon whom Luke bestows special praise because of his exemplary conduct (Lk. 7:1ff.). When comparing the two figures carefully, we can detect the literary artistry of the author who, visually at last, has carefully harmonized both pictures. Both officers are pious, God-fearing, charitable, concerned about their subjects, full of reverence towards the man of God to whom they call for help by means of messengers; and both are granted recognition and salvation.

Again, as so often happens in Luke's writings, there appears a *heavenly visitor*. This visitor is called the " angel of God." No doubt Luke means to indicate a self-revelation of divine will and divine providence. For God speaks to man in accordance with time-conditioned images and concepts. The detail " the ninth hour " is significant. It is a *prayer-hour* observed by the Jews. Presumably the centurion respected this hour of the day. He appears to have belonged to the circle of the so-called " God-fearing." There were many of these in the non-Jewish world. They honored the God of the Jews and professed the Jewish faith, without formally passing over to Judaism. This centurion is, consequently, a man of prayer. And as he prayed, we may assume, this heavenly message was conveyed to him.

"Two of his servants," probably two slaves who served his family, and a soldier whose pious sentiments are especially noteworthy, journey to Joppe with the task of seeking out Simon Peter in the house of Simon the tanner and of asking him to accompany them back to their master in Caesarea. Again *the word of God is being fulfilled.* This is a special characteristic—as we have seen before—of Luke's literary style. The word goes from one city to another—and always under the direction and guidance of the Spirit.

The Instruction to Peter (10:9–23)

⁹On the next day as this little band traveled towards their destination and neared the city, Peter ascended to the rooftop to pray about the sixth hour. ¹⁰Then he became hungry and wanted something to eat; but while it was being prepared for him, he was rapt in ecstasy. ¹¹He saw the heaven opened and a container like a great linen sheet descending, which was let down to the earth by all four corners. In it were all four-footed and creeping animals of the earth and the birds of the air, ¹³and a voice called out to him, " Rise, Peter, slaughter and eat." ¹⁴Peter replied, " Never, never, Lord. For I have never eaten anything common or unclean." ¹⁵And the voice spoke to him again a second time, " What God has made clean, do you dare to call unclean?" ¹⁶This happened three times, and immediately the container was taken up into heaven.

None of the many wonderful events which the Acts of the
Apostles narrates bears so many earmarks of the fabulous, of the
fantastic as this which Peter experienced so personally. On the
other hand, we have no compelling reason to question the *reality
of what Peter experienced,* insofar as we do not on principle
deny the possibility of the parapsychical, that is, the appearance
of the spiritual and the divine world in some tangible form in
this world. Even though certain national characteristics of the
Jewish people may have found their way into the narrative, this
does not justify us looking upon the whole as a sheer symbol or as
the pictorial vesture of an idea.

The church is presented and represented in Peter. And now
the church at *one of the most decisive turning points in her
history.* We have seen how the infant church was intimately
linked to Judaism, and to its religious and cultural practices. So
intimate was this relationship that Saul—in possession of a
warrant and a commission granted him by the supreme authority
among the Jews—was of the opinion that the church should be
treated as an institution related to Judaism and its members proceeded against as apostates from Judaism. Saul experienced the
call from heaven; the Lord himself stood squarely in his path
and pointed out to him the new direction he was to travel. At
that moment the horizon of his work was broadened.

Peter was certain that he was an apostle. In what has preceded
we have viewed him as a person fully conscious of his witness.
But he is *still a Jew,* a Jew in his thoughts and in his activities.
He still feels himself bound to the religious practices of Judaism
for reasons deeply embedded in his purity and faithfulness of
soul. He went up to the rooftop " at the sixth hour " to give himself over to prayer in accordance with Jewish custom. " In the
morning, in the evening, at noon, I will sigh and moan; he

hears my voice," says the pious Jew (Ps. 55:18). As a rigorous servant of the law, Peter complies minutely and conscientiously with the law concerning food; he observes all the distinctions between " clean and unclean " which are so precisely delineated in Mosaic legislation and in rabbinical theology. And in holy protest, he refuses to obey the command given him by the mysterious voice, when he rebelliously cries out, " Never, never, Lord. For I have never eaten anything common or unclean." He voices this with almost unbelievable conviction. His words make us realize how difficult it can be for men to free themselves from structures in which they are raised, even when it is a question of sacrificing the superficial for the essential.

We see Peter involved in just such a situation. He had enjoyed a schooling under the tutelage of Jesus, who had declared, " Not that which enters a man from without defiles him, but rather what comes out of him defiles the man " (Mk. 7:15). He had personally co-experienced how unhesitatingly Jesus betook himself to the home of the gentile centurion of Capharnaum and cured his servant (Lk. 7:6ff.). He was aware of the critical condemnations of the cultural externals of Judaism as we find them listed in the gospel of Luke (11:39ff.). Peter had also personally experienced the miracles of the Holy Spirit and had seen the dawn of the new era of salvation—yet despite all this, he finds it difficult to understand the change and to *emancipate himself from the traditional practices of the Jewish law.*

We are dealing here first with the law restricting the Jews to certain kinds of food, a matter of importance then but today scarcely relevant. It was, however, of great consequence to Peter. He must have recognized it immediately. We know how fanatical Judaism developed and formulated severe strictures in regard to the problem of levitical and cultual uncleanness because of her contacts with the non-Jewish world. Thus *the gentiles were considered unclean.* Because of this prohibition every kind of mixed conviviality with them was frowned upon. How profoundly this problem affected the primitive Christian missionary efforts can be glimpsed in the letters of Paul, especially in the first letter to the Corinthians, where the Apostle tries to prove with all the theological arguments at his command the lawfulness of eating flesh offered to heathen idols (1 Cor. 8–10). And again in the letter to the Galatians, in words filled with emotion, he returns to the same difficulty. He narrates how in Antioch he had to call the attention of the faithful to the fact that both Peter and Barnabas as well as their other followers were emancipated from the ancient prohibition (Gal. 2:1ff.). The matter of eating forbidden flesh and the course to be pursued on the missions were as a consequence intricately dependent one upon the other. And a later passage from the Acts will show how this problem was vitally related to the proclamation of the " good news " to the gentiles.

[17]*Now while Peter tried to explain to himself what the vision which he had seen actually meant, behold the men whom Cornelius had sent, having inquired after Simon's house, stood at the door.* [18]*They called out and inquired whether a stranger by the name of Peter, might be a guest there.* [19]*While Peter pondered on the vision, the Spirit spoke to him, " Look, three men are searching for you.* [20]*Rise, go down and accompany them without hesitation; for I have sent them."* [21]*Then Peter went down to the men and said, " Look, I am he whom you seek. For what reason are you here?"* [22]*They replied, " Cornelius, the centurion, a just and God-fearing man, who is highly respected by all the Jewish people, received instructions from a*

holy angel to invite you to visit him and to listen to the words which you may say to him." ²³Then he invited them to enter, treated them hospitably, and departed with them. Some of the brethren from Joppe also accompanied him.

The *instruction of God* produced an effect on both the participants: on the part of Cornelius and on the part of Peter; they come together now in the house of Simon, the tanner, under the direct guidance of the Spirit in accordance with the plan of God. We are made aware of the progressive stages of knowledge with which Peter obeyed the Spirit's instructions. For in the profoundest sense of the word the deportment of Peter is dictated by an *obedience* which relieves him of all personal judgment and manifests his acceptance of the will of God which is from day to day revealed ever more clearly to him. He realizes that it is not a matter which concerns himself or his own person alone, but regulates the course of the church, subordinated to his own will. All this did not take place without vacillation on his own part; his reluctance is demonstrated by his initial refusal and his original protest against obeying the command to eat of the various animals; but it is also shown by his brooding and pondering twice mentioned (10:17, 19). And it is again the Spirit who intervenes and urges him to accompany " unhesitatingly " those who had been sent by the centurion. " Unhesitatingly," says the Spirit. We are scarcely able to experience today what this word demanded of Peter. When later on we are confronted with the unrest which this innocent accompaniment aroused in the Christian community in Jerusalem, still faithful to the law (11:1f.), we are enabled to gain some inkling of Peter's courage and of the sentiments which welled up within him.

Peter clearly recognized the keynote of the message: "I have sent them." He can detect the voice of the Risen Lord, of the same Lord who had called and sent his apostles to be witnesses. And as so often before while in the company of the pre-paschal Lord, so now Peter submits obediently to command. What did he say on that occasion on the lake of Genesareth when Jesus ordered him to launch out into the deep and let down his nets to catch some fish which until then had eluded him? "Master, we have labored the whole night through and have caught nothing; but at your word, I will let down the nets" (Lk. 5:5).

He stood before the three men from Caesarea. He listened to their story. Here a detail is added to the original message of the angel: "to listen to the words which you may say." Precisely this detail is of special importance for Peter, for he is given the impression that *he has been called as mediator,* as a preacher of a message. "We must obey God rather than men" (5:29), as he said on a previous occasion when he had faced the Sanhedrin. Now he treated the new arrivals hospitably and set out with them. It was a daring step to receive the gentiles into the church; it was an equally daring decision to set out with such companions to visit the gentiles.

The church went along with Peter on the road from Joppe to Caesarea. The "brothers of Joppe" who accompanied him are at the same time perceptive of a resolute and fundamental change. According to 11:12 there were six persons who made up his escort. They would be witnesses of whatever would take place in Caesarea. And it was important that they be present. Again the human element of the church plays its own peculiar and individual role. And Peter can rely on these "six brothers" and their testimony to justify his actions, as this will soon become increasingly necessary.

THE ENCOUNTER WITH CORNELIUS (10:24-33)

[24]*On the next day he arrived in Caesarea. Cornelius was waiting for them: and he had invited his relatives and close friends.* [25]*As Peter sought to enter, Cornelius went out to meet him and in veneration fell at his feet.* [26]*But Peter raised him up and said: " Stand up! I, too, am only a human being."* [27]*And speaking with him, he entered the house and found a great number of people gathered there, and he said to them, " You know that it is unlawful for a Jew to associate with non-Jews or to enter their homes. God, however, has shown me not to hold any man to be unholy or unclean.* [29]*For this reason, when I was sent for, I came without raising any objection. So I ask now: Why did you send for me?"*

After what has been said, this scene requires no explanation. What emerges with almost dramatic impressiveness is the *profound desire for salvation evinced by Cornelius.* He had awaited the arrival of Peter. Paganism as an entity, as personified, so to speak, in this Roman officer, waits for the message and for the gift of salvation. This scene will be repeated frequently throughout the history of the Christian missions. For among the gentiles there were seekers, fashioned after the spiritual model of Cornelius. Thus we should avoid looking upon the paganism which the early church encountered within the framework of Hellenism as being purely polytheistic. Much genuine spirituality and a benevolent humanity are to be found in it. This was a ploughed and fertile field for the word of the gospel, much better prepared and much more receptive to the message in many respects than the inflexible legalism of Judaism! We are reminded of Jesus' words to the official from Capharnaum: " I say to you: not once have I found in Jerusalem one with such great faith " (Lk. 7:9).

The centurion greets Peter. And he did so by employing one of the most abject forms of greeting current in that age, namely, by means of *proskynesis*. Had he ever done it before to any human being? Through it the adoration of the Divine Being himself was in general outwardly expressed. He recognizes in Peter something more than purely natural, though the concept of what he actually represented may not have been clear in his own mind. Peter decisively but kindly declines this mark of veneration. " Stand up! I, too, am only a human being." We cannot know, of course, whether at that moment he recalled how he himself had thrown himself at the feet of another and had stammered out the words, " Depart from me, Lord, for I am a sinful man " (Lk. 5:8); or whether there had raced through his mind that other scene in the courtyard of Caiaphas where as a man he had so miserably failed his master. Now a Roman centurion bends his knees before him and throws himself at his feet. He cannot bear it; he declines such a mark of honor. In this we are given a lesson: that the church must always retrace her steps to the unassuming Peter.

Peter greets the assembled company. He surveyed a scene which was unfamiliar to him. It must also have been strange to the company itself, to see a Jew approach them on familiar terms, They were well aware of the reserve of the Jews in the presence of strangers. They knew of their religious intolerance; they knew too of the religious wall which they had built around themselves. Peter seized upon this thought and explained to them the reason why he was in their midst. He is no longer concerned about the question of permissible or forbidden food, but about the more essential problem of a world-wide mission. The Jewish distinction between "clean" and "unclean" no longer exists for him. The barriers which have prevented the church from pressing forward into the domain of the gentiles have all been broken down. And Paul, whose calling is recounted with good reason, will be the one who will traverse a daring and resolute course and overcome what remains of the last obstacles.

[30]*Cornelius answered, "Four days ago at this very hour, I was in my house, praying, and behold a man stood before me in bright garments and* [31]*said, 'Cornelius, your prayers have been heard and your alms have been remembered by God.* [32]*Send now to Joppe and have Simon with the surname Peter come to you; he lodges in the house of Simon the tanner, near the sea.'* [33]*So then I sent for you at once, and you came and you have done rightly by coming. Now we are all present in the sight of God, to learn all with which you were tasked by the Lord."*

Peter again learns of *the instruction which had been given by our Lord*. Cornelius himself tells of his own personal experience. In conformity with the imaginary literary mannerism of the non-Jewish world, the angel is depicted as "a man in bright garments." Again we learn that the heavenly visitor appeared during the time that Cornelius was sunk in prayer. The impression is given that the appearance of the figure bathed in light is a direct answer of heaven to the request of the man praying, for we read —in a somewhat freer rendering of the angel's words (in contrast to 10:4)—that "your prayer has been heard and your alms have been remembered by God." For what did the centurion pray? He was a seeker. For the enlightenment of the Spirit, for the way of truth and of salvation—these must have been his intentions.

Now the way is shown to him. He expresses a joyful readiness in his words: " Now we are all present in the sight of God to learn all that with which you were tasked by God." The message of the gospel comes to him and to all who are gathered around him. This is genuine community—*a remarkable community of catechumens,* such as will over and over again be drawn together for the messengers of the faith, ready for instruction. They are gathered together " in the sight of God." This fact sets this community apart from all others. Cornelius recognizes the mission and the fullness of power which Peter possessed: " all that with which you were tasked by the Lord," he says to him. He testifies to the plenitude of power which the church possesses. To her is entrusted the word of salvation for a valid and binding mediatorship.

The Reply of Peter (10:34–43)

[34]*Then Peter opened his mouth and said, " Now I know in truth that God is not a respecter of persons,* [35]*and that every person who fears him and practices justice is acceptable to him.* [36]*He has delivered his message to the children of Israel and proclaimed to them peace through Jesus Christ. He is the Lord above all.* [37]*You know of everything that has happened throughout the whole of Judea, beginning in Galilee, after the baptism which John preached:* [38]*how God had anointed Jesus of Nazareth with the Holy Spirit and with power and how he went about the country, doing good and driving out the devil from all those who were possessed; for God was with him,* [39]*and we are witnesses to all that he did in the territory of the Jews and in Jerusalem, he whom they killed by hanging him to a tree.* [40]*God*

raised him up on the third day and he appeared, [41]not to all the people, but to us, the witnesses foreordained by God, we who ate and drank with him after his resurrection from the dead. [42]He charged us with the task of preaching and testifying to the people that he is ordained by God to judge the living and the dead. [43]All the prophets bear witness that through the invocation of his name, all who believe in him will obtain the remission of their sins."

This sermon of Peter to Cornelius and to the group gathered around him is offered to us by Luke in a concise summary form, and presents to us the *basic thoughts in the proclamation of the " good news " to a non-Jewish audience.* In comparison to the missionary sermons of the evangelist which we have seen thus far, the proof from sacred scripture is relegated to the background, although unmistakable overtones of Old Testament terminology permeate the entire sermon. In the foreground Luke places the salvific activity of Jesus of Nazareth and the authorization and verification of his mission by his deeds, especially by his resurrection from the dead. The apostle speaks as an ambassador of this Jesus Christ, the Lord of the universe, and he points out the way to salvation, namely, by a return through faith in him by men.

The words of introduction themselves as used by Peter have a profound significance: " God is not a respecter of persons." This is an allusion to 1 Samuel 16:7. In this passage the Lord says to Samuel, " Do not look at his appearance or at the height of his stature; for I have rejected him because I see not as men see. Men look at outward appearances; the Lord, however, looks at the heart." A high degree of sense data is bound up in these words. It is explained in a salvation-historic way. In his proffer of salvation, God does not pay heed to those things by which men are attracted. Before him, distinctions of social standing or of sex or of race or of people possess no meaning; he does not take into account even the distinction of religious belief—and in this fact there is a thought which disturbs Peter and bewilders him no end. "And in every nation anyone who fears him and practices justice is acceptable to him." We understand correctly these unheard-of, courageous words. They are not used to favor religious indifference, certainly not in the sense of a religious indifferentism. Peter is expressing the way of salvation preached by the church, in whose name he speaks. He wishes to say of *this way of salvation* that it is without exception open and accessible to all who await its advent with reverence for the mystery of God, while searching for it according to justice and righteousness.

And now Peter directs the attention of his listeners to the unique history of the harbinger of peace and " Lord over all." The *content of the gospels* is here compressed into the smallest possible compass. " You know everything that happened throughout the whole of Judea," he is able to say. This turn of expression apparently does not assume that Cornelius and his group knew of the events connected with the life and death of Jesus from Christian sources, from Christian messengers of faith. For the assumption that Philip had arrived in Caesarea some time before the coming of Peter, as some have concluded from verse 8:40, is far from certain. Peter presupposes much more, namely, that a person could have received direct information of the events connected with Jesus in Caesarea itself, where, moreover, the seat of the Roman governor was located. For us it has a bearing; it witnesses to the fact that already in his lifetime Jesus was the object of serious scrutiny and was more than a mere passing sensation. We should recall that Paul himself when testifying before King Agrippa declared openly, " The king whom I address with such boldness knows about these things. I am convinced that none of these things are unknown to him; for this was done not in some neglected corner " (26:26).

Peter next expatiates on the incomparable conduct of this genuine benefactor and puissant saviour. He has a reason for speaking as he does. " We are witnesses to all that he did in the territory of the Jews and in Jerusalem." Peter includes *the witness of all* in the one word " we "—*the witness of all those* who " were together during all the time that the Lord Jesus went in and out among us, from the baptism of John down to the day on which he was taken up " (1:21). And again we are impressed by the grave concern which he seeks to express in his apostolic sermons, namely, to base the " good news " of salvation on the trustworthiness of his own historical personal experience.

And here again the death and resurrection of Jesus stand out as the decisive event in man's salvation. And again the witnesses of the resurrection offer their own proofs. They have seen him; in fact, they were permitted to share a meal with him. The gospel of Luke, as well as that of John, apprise us of the fact that the Risen One partook of food. This act is mysterious and inexplicable, for it is entirely alien to common experience and to the teaching of theology : how a transfigured body is able to eat and to drink. In these circumstances this was, however, a sign that the disciples had actually enjoyed the company of the Lord. This sharing in a common meal continues, moreover, in the liturgical celebration of the Lord's Supper, even though in the unique form of a sacramental reality. The salvific mission of the church is based on the experience of the resurrection and on the encounter of disciples with the Risen Lord. For this event is oriented to the salvific experience of the whole world. The faith of the apostles and of the early church impelled them *to carry the message of the Lord* to mankind. Peter says to Cornelius, " He charged us with the task of preaching and of testifying to the people that it is he who is ordained to judge the living and the dead." We know of this commission from Christ's command to preach to the whole world (1 : 8) and also from Luke's gospel (Lk. 24 : 24ff.), where it is summarized as an instruction of our Lord. There we also read the substantive sentence, " Penance and the forgiveness of sins should be proclaimed in his name to all peoples—beginning from Jerusalem " (Lk. 24:47). When Peter, as a consequence, speaks to Cornelius about " the people," he could scarcely have intended to restrict his preaching of the gospel solely to the Jews, but must have willed to include in his scope all men. Or did Peter wish to say that although the mission to preach to all nations was meant first of all in regard to the Jews, now God himself intervenes in a special way to provide the gentiles with the message of salvation, the proclamation of " good news "? The text furnishes no data for such a conclusion.

It may come as a surprise to us that Peter designates Jesus, the *judge of the living and the dead,* as the essential content of the " good news." In these words we can discern an earlier formula which was inserted into the *credo* of the early church. It is interesting to note that in Paul's speech in the Areopagus, which resembles this sermon of Peter, he speaks also of the judgeship of Jesus, as when he says, " For God has fixed the day on which the earth will be judged in accordance with his righteousness by a man whom he has commissioned and accredited for it, by raising him from the dead " (17:31). Resurrection and judgeship are related in closest kinship.

For Jesus is both judge and saviour at one and the same time.

First he performs his salvific service, before he exercises his office as judge. Purposely, then, when Peter uses the phrase "*forgiveness of sins,*" in order to summarize the entire salvific activity of Jesus, he stresses the fact that the oracles of past centuries emphasized this point by means of the voices of the prophets.

THE WITNESS OF THE SPIRIT—BAPTISM OF THE GENTILES (10:44-48)

⁴⁴While Peter was still speaking, the Holy Spirit descended upon all who listened to his words. ⁴⁵The faithful among the circumcised who had accompanied Peter were astonished that the gift of the Holy Spirit was poured out over the gentiles; ⁴⁶for they heard how they spoke in tongues and had glorified God. ⁴⁷Then Peter began to speak and say, " Would there be anyone who would refuse to give us water, so that these could not be baptized who have received the Holy Spirit, even as we?" ⁴⁸And he gave the order that they should be baptized in the name of Jesus Christ. Thereupon they besought him to stay with them for a few days.

The story of Cornelius is unique both insofar as divine providence and divine guidance are concerned. Only on such a supposition can we fully understand the events as they took place. God himself bears witness to the significant change of procedure that has occurred in the work of salvation by means of Peter's encounter with the centurion, Cornelius. He himself utters the Amen to the speech of his ambassador. Just as at Pentecost in Jerusalem the risen and exalted Lord had revealed himself through *the coming of the Holy Spirit* and through the speeches in divers tongues to demonstrate to mankind the beginning of the salvific labors of the church, so now at Capharnaum in the house of Cornelius, the centurion, there takes place another, *a new Pentecost*; it is the symbol of a new beginning: the task of preaching the faith to the gentiles.

Again men are moved by the breathing of the Spirit. They " speak in tongues " and " glorify God." These are men who have not as yet been baptized; they are struck to the very depths of their being by the news of salvation which Peter announces to them. They are men who are honestly searching for the truth and manifest a readiness of soul; they know that salvation has been promised to them. " While Peter was still speaking, the Holy Spirit descended upon all who listened to his words." Is this not an allusion to the *salvific importance of the word?* Of that word spoken by God's ambassadors who are filled with the fullness of the Spirit? Of that word which is now capable of being heard? The significance of this new pentecostal mystery at Caesarea is to be found chiefly *in its character as a sign* for Peter and for the church that they acted correctly in proceeding towards Caesarea, to the centurion who awaited them.

Justification in Jerusalem (11:1–18)

REPROACHES BY THE PRIMITIVE COMMUNITY (11:1–3)

[1]Now the apostles and the brethren in Judea heard that even the gentiles had accepted the word of God. [2]So when Peter went up to Jerusalem, some of the circumcised expressed their misgivings and said, [3]" You visited the uncircumcised and ate with them."

It would certainly have been unusual if misgivings and criticism had not been voiced after what had happened in Caesarea. For the members of the infant community must surely have regarded the report of events as incredible: *" The gentiles have accepted the word of God."* This news passed from mouth to mouth. We have already read about one such report: " When the apostles, who were in Jerusalem, heard that Samaria had received the word of God, they sent Peter and John to them " (8: 14). Even then it proved to be a startling communiqué to learn that the semi-heathen Samaritans had turned to Christ. " To accept the word of God " is a profound description of the devout reception of the message of salvation preached by Christ. And now the almost unbelievable announcement reaches them that the gentiles—and, we may note by way of addition, even the Romans, who belonged to the forces of occupation—had received baptism. And this time, however, they were unable to despatch members officially commissioned by the community to protect their rights. Because of all this we are conscious—in accordance with the purpose of the Acts—that something incredible and portentous had taken place in Caesarea.

The accentuation of the notions *circumcision and uncircumcised* attests to the fact that regarding the affair at Caesarea we are dealing with the judaizing intelligentsia among the community members. They are not without reason called " some of the circumcised." Paul employs the same expression in his letter to the Galatians (2: 12) when he mentions that in Antioch, Peter withdrew from a common table with the gentiles " out of fear for those who were circumcised." " You visited with the uncircumcised and ate with them " was the reproach hurled at Peter when he returned to Jerusalem. This attitude afforded the early church one of the severest obstacles she had to overcome. Let us now see how Peter and through him the church confronted this very problem.

THE ANSWER OF PETER (11:4–18)

Then Peter began to explain from beginning to end, and then he said, ⁵" I was in the city of Joppe and I prayed; then like a great sheet a cloth was let down from heaven by its four corners, and it reached to me. ⁶I looked inside; I examined it and saw the four-footed beasts of the earth, the wild and the creeping animals and the birds of the air. ⁷I also heard a voice speaking to me: ' Rise, Peter, kill and eat.' I answered, ' Never, never, Lord; for never has anything common or unclean ever entered into my mouth.' ⁹In answer the voice from heaven spoke a second time: ' What God has made clean, you should not call unclean.' ¹⁰This happened three times and then everything was drawn back up to heaven, ¹¹and behold, immediately three men stood before the house in which we were staying; they had been sent to me from Caesarea. ¹²The Spirit then bade me that I should without hesitation accompany them. These six brethren also went with me, and we entered the house of this man. ¹³He reported to us how he had seen the angel who had entered his house and said, ' Send to Joppe and have Simon surnamed Peter come to you; ¹⁴he will say things to you, by which salvation will come upon you and upon your household.' ¹⁵When I began to speak, the Holy Spirit descended upon them, as he did upon all of us the first time. ¹⁶Then I remembered the word of the Lord, saying, ' John baptized with water, you shall be baptized with the Holy Spirit ' (1:15). ¹⁷If God had imparted to them the same gift which he had to us, because they believed in Jesus Christ, how could I be in a position to place limits on God? " [18]*When they heard this, their minds were set at ease and they praised God and said, " Thus God has also bestowed upon the gentiles a change of heart, leading to life."*

It is worthy of note that in this long passage there is repeated in detail everything which had already been presented in the previous narrative. We recognize in this the essence of the literary style of Luke. To him it is important to imprint indelibly upon the reader, in as vivid terms as possible, the most decisive events in the history of the early church. We have already pointed out a similar literary artifice in the narrative recounting the call of Saul-Paul and in the story of Cornelius.

Peter had left himself wide open for an obvious rebuke. He again makes clear to the community that he had undergone a personal experience that was as shattering for himself as it was for them. Was it necessary for him as head of the community to give such an accounting? For had he not undertaken the journey to Lydda and Joppe only as an emissary of the community of Jerusalem? It would perhaps be more correct to look upon this affair not so much as a matter which touches upon the constitutional structure of the church, but rather as an evidence of the *guidance of the Spirit,* to which not only Peter but also the other apostles were subject. The apostle and the community realized full well that they were most intimately united together in the mystery of the body of Christ without detriment to the hierarchical structure which traces its origin back to Christ. This order assigns to the apostleship a task which transcends that of the community, but at the same time a task which must be accomplished for and within the community.

Antioch and the First Gentile Community (11:19–30)

The story of Cornelius was an indication of the decisive step which the church had taken into the pagan world. Now we can perceive the broad domain of the forward-striding message of the church, and we are reminded again of Stephen—of the persecution which ended with his witness in blood and with his death. In such retrospect we can better appreciate how closely interwoven were those events of which we learned after the election of the seven (6:1ff.). For this reason we considered that the second era of the church began with 6:1 onward. Now it is necessary for the author again to turn back to the outbreak of the persecution in order to make clear the connection between the many events related in his narrative.

The Persecuted as Messengers of the Gospel (11:19–21)

¹⁹*Now those, who as a result of the persecution which began with Stephen, were scattered, came by various roads to Phoenicia and Cyprus and Antioch, where they proclaimed the word only to the Jews.* ²⁰*There were among them some men from Cyprus and Cyrene who on their arrival in Antioch, spoke also to the Greeks and proclaimed the message of Jesus, the Lord.* ²¹*And the hand of the Lord was with them; a great number became believers and were converted to the Lord.*

These introductory remarks are concerned not only with the question of a possible chronological order, but also and chiefly with the proof of the causal connection between *the persecution of the church* and her internal and *external growth*. The persecuted, among whom was the group gathered around the seven, become witnesses and ambassadors of the gospel which is persecuted through and in them. Phoenicia and Cyprus are singled out as the scene of the mission which is to be established, and special emphasis is also given to the city of Antioch in Syria. But why Antioch? According to an ancient tradition Luke was a native of Antioch. This city was after Rome and Alexandria the third largest city in the Roman Empire, a cosmopolitan community not only of economic importance but also of cultural and religious significance. The spread of the Christian message in that city consequently denotes another memorable advance forward in carrying the " word " to and through the world.

In contrast to the conversion of Cornelius which took place privately and in the realm of the personal, that in Antioch was in the realm of the public and the communal: *the first gentile Christian community is established.* Antioch becomes, in a grand manner, the center and the starting-point of the mission to the gentiles. And even though, in spite of everything, Jerusalem will continue to retain the honor and distinction of being the mother community and will not cease to enjoy the deepest respect of the entire church, from now on Antioch will assume the role which Jerusalem had enjoyed up to this point.

These men, therefore, from Cyprus and Cyrene, who as ambassadors of the faith contacted the Hellenists, that is, the non-Jews, set into motion an extremely important piece of machinery for the history of the church. " They proclaimed to them the message of Jesus, the Lord." The shortest summary of apostolic preaching is expressed in the formula: " Jesus, the Lord," " Jesus, the *Kyrios*." These words are a confession of faith. We became aware of this already when Peter preached his first sermon on Pentecost: " With all certainty the whole house of Israel recognized: God has made this Jesus the Lord and the Messiah, whom you have crucified " (2:36). And when in his

letters Paul uses the title *Kyrios* to describe the honor which
Jesus enjoys, he is conscious that by it and with it he embraces
in one word the entire mysterious power and grandeur of the
Exalted Christ. In his letter to the Romans, he writes, " If you
confess with your lips ' Lord Jesus ' and believe in your heart
that God raised him from the dead, you will be saved " (10:9).
And in his first letter to the Corinthians we read, " No one can
say: Lord, Jesus, except by the Holy Spirit " (12:3). And we
know well the truly shattering nature of the statement concerning the *Kyrios* that is found in the unique, profound confession
of faith in Christ in the letter to the Philippians: " And for this
reason God has so highly exalted him and bestowed upon him a
name which is above all other names, that at the name of Jesus
every knee should bend of those in heaven, of those on earth, of
those under the earth, and every tongue will confess: ' Jesus
Christ is Lord, for the glorification of the Father ' " (Phil.
2:9–11).

So in the simple phrase " Jesus, the Lord " there is included
whatever faith is capable of enunciating concerning him. Precisely the non-Jew was receptive of this message; the confession
of faith in Jesus as Lord became formally a password; it counter-
acted the claims of many other " Lords " who were worshipped
by divers cults of those times. " The good news " of Christ
among the Hellenists of Antioch attained great success. " The
hand of the Lord " was with those who for the first time under-
took to proclaim the gospel to the gentiles. The Holy Spirit collaborated with them. The first gentile Christian community is
now in existence in this world. There is inaugurated a new
church, which no longer appears to be what it had been in the
past, a sect of Judaism.

Barnabas and Saul in Antioch (11:22–26)

[22]*The report reached the ears of the community in Jerusalem and they sent Barnabas to Antioch.* [23]*When he reached there and saw the grace of God, he rejoiced and exhorted them all to remain faithful with resolute hearts to the Lord.* [24]*For he was a venerable man, filled with the Holy Spirit and full of faith; and a still greater number of people were won over to the Lord.* [25]*Then he set out and took the road to Tarsus to seek out Paul, and when he found him, he brought him with him to Antioch.* [26]*And it came to pass that they actually worked together in Antioch for a full year and they instructed many persons in doctrine. And it was in Antioch that the disciples received the name Christians for the first time.*

It was to be expected that the growth of the community in Antioch would attract the attention of the mother community in Jerusalem and of the ecclesiastical authorities there. For the community there felt itself responsible for whatever took place in the Christian missionary field. Its concern for the unity of faith and the purity of doctrine, for a profound unanimity in both, was the driving force behind its anxiety. The news about the establishment of a gentile Christian community must surely have deeply touched that church which up to that point had been composed exclusively of Judeo-Christian members and of a corresponding cult.

Therefore, *they sent Barnabas to Antioch.* Peter was still, perhaps, on his way through Palestine. And Barnabas appeared to be the man best fitted for the task, one especially called for it, since it demanded great trust in God. " Men from Cyprus and Cyrene " were those who had ventured to take the initiative by establishing a mission among the " Hellenists " of Antioch. Barnabas knew them perhaps personally. He, too, traced his origin to Cyprus (4 : 36). And not only that : he was " a venerable man, filled with the Holy Spirit and full of faith." The one who wrote this description is Luke, the Antiochian, who, as we have already seen, entertained great respect for Barnabas. Barnabas was not a member of the twelve, but he enjoyed such great esteem that the Acts of the Apostles twice bestows upon him the title " apostle " (14 : 4, 14). It was Barnabas, as we have already mentioned, in whom Paul encountered the first representative of the " governing church."

Barnabas came upon another field, blessed by God and ripe for the harvest. He " rejoiced when he reached there and saw the grace of God." Our text names as the *grace of God* the work which the messengers of the faith had performed in Antioch. This is a very meaningful statement : " Grace " is ransom for the " law." In Paul's letter to the Romans, he writes, " Justified by faith we have peace with God through our Lord Jesus Christ, through whom we have access by faith to this grace, in which we now stand " (Rom. 5 : 1ff.). And in the same letter he states, " You are not under the law, but under grace " (Rom. 6 : 14). These texts remind us also of the prologue to John's gospel : " The law was given us through Moses ; grace and truth came to us through Jesus Christ " (Jn. 1 : 17). Salvation in Christ is pure grace, nothing but grace. This is true for the Jew who was converted to Christ, but much more strikingly for the non-Jew. Barnabas was conscious of this fact when he saw the church in Antioch in the process of construction. We can understand the " joy " which pervaded him, when confronted by the activity of grace ; he could only exhort them to " remain faithful to God." Possibly by rendering the text literally we could say : " to remain with the Lord." Jesus is the " Lord " to whom the community of Antioch had dedicated itself.

Barnabas had not let Paul slip from his mind. He started for and journeyed to Tarsus to seek him out. We read this brief account, therefore, with mixed feelings. Where is Paul? As we saw, he was forced to flee, as it were, from Jerusalem after his first encounter with the community there. At the time, " the brothers " rid themselves of him by shipping him back to Tarsus (9:23-30). We do not know precisely how many years have passed since this banishment. Our text speaks of him as one lost and forgotten, when and if his name is mentioned. The community in Jerusalem does not appear to have grieved at his absence. Perhaps it may have rejoiced, as can easily happen, when natures more forceful and emotional than ordinary cause unrest in a group which hitherto had enjoyed a tranquil peace. How Paul busied himself during those years of absence we do not know. Perhaps he was even entirely inactive during the whole time.

Barnabas, however, had not forgotten him. It was he who had on that previous occasion in Jerusalem mediated the trust and the confidence with which the mother community regarded the refugee from Damascus and bore witness to Saul's encounter with God (9:27). The Acts of the Apostles gives us no hint as to what source Barnabas had gone to gain his information about Paul, yet *the friendship of these two men* was and remained an arrangement under the Spirit which guided the church and the welfare of the community.

Both these men collaborated for a " full year " in Antioch. The community grew as a result of their labors. But we may assume that much more took place in that year than a mere increase in the number of the faithful or a strengthening of the ecclesiastical life of the community. Both for Paul and for Barnabas it was a year in which insights were acquired and skills attained. Equipped with these, both would soon depart for the work to be performed on the missions on a grand scale and with a high degree of proficiency. The loosening of those ties by which the Jewish concept of the law still enslaved the infant community to Judaism and posed an obstacle to all its activities, was now more closely recognized and more fully analyzed. In this same year Paul determined the means he was to take in order to become a full preacher of Christian salvation, of grace and of freedom in Christ.

Help for Jerusalem (11:27–30)

²⁷*In those days prophets came down from Jerusalem to Antioch,* ²⁸*and one of them by the name of Agabas arose and by the power of the Spirit predicted that there would be a great famine all over the world; this took place in the days of Claudius.* ²⁹*Then the disciples decided that every one of them should, if he were in a position to do so, send something for the relief of the brothers living in Judea.* ³⁰*This they did and they sent it to the priests by the hand of Barnabas and Saul.*

In many respects this short notice is of interest for the picture we have of the early church, for in it there is given us a moving example of the brisk connections existing between the mother community of Jerusalem and the Christian community of the diaspora. For very understandable reasons the early church manifested a particular regard and lively concern for the gentile mission in Antioch. " Prophets from Jerusalem " arrived in

Antioch: thus for the very first time in the Acts of the Apostles we learn about *Christian prophets.* They were as much a part of the early church as were the prophets of the Old Testament, a part of the people, the chosen people of God. Their position in the community and the tasks they performed, translated into Christian terms, were practically the same as those ascribed to the Old Testament prophets. They cannot, however, be inserted into any predetermined or extant ecclesiastical hierarchy. For the charism of prophecy, even though it was possessed in most instances by the officials of the church, traced its origin to a direct and an immediate divine vocation. The purpose which they served was not simply to proffer insight into the future, but also to furnish every sort of admonition and directive for the way of salvation.

The famine, foretold by Agabas and noted by Luke, actually took place under the Emperor Claudius (A.D. 41–54). This is attested to by non-biblical sources, at least in the sense that under this emperor the great provinces of the empire were ravaged by famine at various times. In this connection it is worthwhile noting that the Jewish historian Flavius Josephus recounts that under the Roman governors Fadus and Tiberius Alexander (A.D. 44–48), a severe famine broke out in Judea. We would venture the opinion that it was this famine which Agabas prophesied, since chronological considerations would seem to harmonize with the prophesied event.

The committee at Antioch resolved to be of active assistance to the suffering community. As a result of their resolution we find a report of the *first collection* ever taken up by a minor community for the support of the mother community. We are, in addition, shown another feature of the image we call the church. This collection becomes a model for all future relief activities upon which the church will embark on behalf of her needy brethren everywhere. In the community of goods, already described and practiced by the infant community, we can observe the spirit of charity and union which impelled the infant community to forgo the possession of personal and private property. To Paul more than to the others was granted the incomparable gift of combining economic concern for the mother community with untiring efforts levied by his apostolic labors. From his letters we learn how at the same time the Apostle was exercised about divorcing this financial work of the church from everything that might prove to be beyond his resources or scandalous to the faithful. He who had urged the right to be supported by the community (1 Cor. 9:6) generally, personally renounced it, and the work of his own hands earned enough for what was necessary either for himself or for his companions.

The Persecution of the Church by Herod Agrippa
(12:1–25)

An important segment of the Acts is concluded by chapter 12, and in the next chapter our attention is directed to another theme: the missionary labors of Paul. If we divided the first twelve chapters into two parts, we did so because they formed a homogeneous whole in contrast to the content of chapters 13–28. The course of the church from Jerusalem to Antioch was spread before our eyes in various individual incidents and in "collective" narratives. Once again, at their conclusion, we are shown Jerusalem and the community present there as being under the guidance of the apostles. Once again, Peter passes before us, the same Peter with whose person the church up to the present has so personally and so intimately been engaged. Once again—since it fits in so well with the previous image of the church—we are shown persecutions and threats, yet reminded of the constant help of God and the invincibility of the activity of the Spirit—which becomes especially visible for us in the agonizing death of the persecutor by which this section is concluded.

The Miraculous Liberation of Peter (12:1–17)

IN PRISON (12:1–4)

[1]*About that time King Herod stirred up trouble, so that he could with evil intent proceed against the members of the community.* [2]*He had James, the brother of John, beheaded.* [3]*When he saw that this pleased the Jews, he went still further and had Peter apprehended—these were the days of the unleavened bread.* [4]*After he had seized him, he threw him into prison and entrusted his guard to four groups, each of four soldiers, with the intention of trying him before the people after the pasch.*

The name Herod awakens unhappy memories when it is mentioned in connection with the history of Jesus and the church. We know of Herod the Great who sought the life of the child of Bethlehem. During the public life of Christ, a Herod was the tetrarch of Galilee and Perea; he was one of the sons of Herod I, and was named Herod Antipas. John the Baptist fell a victim to his whims (Mk. 6:14ff.). He also played a unique role in the trial of Jesus (Lk. 24:8). And now another Herod attracts our attention, a grandson of Herod I. He is called Herod

Agrippa I. As a favorite of Caligula, the Emperor of Rome, from A.D. 37 on his power increased until finally between 41–44 he ruled as king over the entire territory of his grandfather.

THE LIBERATION (12:5–12)

⁵So Peter was consequently held in prison. Prayers were without ceasing offered for him by the community. ⁶That very night before the day when Herod wished to bring him before the people, Peter, chained by two chains, was sleeping between two soldiers, and sentries stood at the gates, guarding the prison. ⁷And behold, an angel of the Lord entered, and a light filled the cell. He nudged Peter in the side, awakened him, and said, " Get up quickly!" The chains fell from his hands. ⁸And the angel said to him, " Dress yourself and put on your sandals." He did this. The angel then said to him further, " Put on your cloak and follow me." ⁹He went out and followed him, but he did not know what was happening to him was real and was done by an angel; he thought that he was having a vision. ¹⁰They passed by the first and the second watchmen and came to the iron gate, which led into the city. This opened of itself and they then passed through it and proceeded further up one of the streets, and immediately the angel disappeared from his side. ¹¹Then Peter came to himself and said, " Now I know for a fact: the Lord sent his angel and rescued me from the hand of Herod and from the expectations of the Jewish people." ¹²When he realized this, he went to the house of Mary, the mother of John by surname Mark, where many were gathered together and were praying.

A *picture of the praying church* is presented here in contrast to what is underscored in the two other rescue stories, and this as a consequence makes it the more meaningful. " Many were gathered together and praying " in the house of the mother of John-Mark, which probably even in Jesus' time was already sacrosanct and afforded a place of refuge for the community. We can say, possibly without fear of contradiction, that in other parts of the world other groups came together to pray for the release of their leader who was imprisoned and threatened with a fate which could only be death. " They prayed without ceasing to God for him "—so Luke begins his narrative of the growth of the church (1 : 12ff.) with an image of a church at prayer. Over and over again he will speak of this fact, namely, that the faithful came together to pray, and that word and deed accompanied the church as she made her fateful journey through the world. Now he is content to show us the power of the praying church; and he does this in an especially impressive fashion. We recall in this connection how precisely in his own gospel he presented and inculcated the necessity and the power of confident prayer—as in the example of the importunate friend (Lk. 11 : 5–8), or the father and his pleading son (Lk. 11 : 11–13), or prayer which should never slacken (Lk. 8 : 1–8).

The presentation of the story of Peter's rescue from prison, which goes into the minutest details, requires no special explanation. The extreme precautions taken in guarding the imprisoned apostle are purposely delineated so graphically in order to portray as clearly as possible the marvelousness of the miracle which was worked and the utter superiority of divine power over the purely human. The " light " which streamed into the darkened cell is a symbol of the presence of God. And when the angel betrays concern over each and every article of clothing which belonged to Peter, this is an indication of how divine providence is concerned about everything which is necessary for man. It is said purposely that the apostle first became aware of the reality of what was happening only after the angel had disappeared.

RETURN TO THE COMMUNITY AND A FAREWELL (12:13–17)

¹³When he knocked on the door of the gateway, a maidservant by the name of Rhoda went to listen, ¹⁴and when she recognized the voice of Peter, she did not open the door but ran back and informed all who were present: " Peter is at the door." ¹⁵They, however, said to her, "You are out of your mind." But she assured them that it was so. Then they said, " It is his angel! " ¹⁶Peter, however, continued to knock; they opened the door, and saw him and were besides themselves with joyous amazement. ¹⁷He made a sign with his hand for them to be silent, related to them how the Lord had brought him out of prison, and said, " Tell this to James and the brothers! " Then he left them and went to another place.

Peter stands at the door of the house with which he had been familiar for so long a time. He knows Mary, the mother of John-Mark; he knew all the people who had congregated there and were still praying—for him. He mentions this same Mark again later on when he writes, ". . . sends you greetings . . . and so does Mark, my son " (1 Pet. 5: 13), and so bears witness to the spiritual bond which links him to the house of Mary. This is that same Mark who as tradition informs us will formulate from the sermons of Peter that gospel which we know of under his name and whose Petrine ancestry is unmistakably recognizable. The church of Christ is not alien to or estranged from all earthly, human relationships or natural ties; she needed then and continues to need, at critical periods of her life among men, communities of brothers and sisters, communities of men and women who are related by blood relationship. This is demonstrated to us in the example of Peter standing at the gateway, knocking at the door, seeking admittance. This is also demonstrated to us by Rhoda, the maidservant, rushing to the door and immediately recognizing the voice of Peter, but letting him stand without so that she could bring the almost incomprehensible news to his friends within.

"You are out of your mind," they say at first. "It is his angel" is their next retort. By acting as they did, they bear witness to the faith which was professed by Judaism, namely, that the heavenly guardian spirit whom God grants to men as associates along life's way not only bears a close resemblance to, but actually is the exact counterpart of the person to whom he has been assigned. Faith in guardian angels was introduced into the teaching of the church from out of this context. What commotion and excitement must have prevailed in that house as the assembled group listened to the knocking at the door, as the visitor continued to make his presence known! They threw the door open and were filled with amazement at what they saw. Peter is surrounded and encircled by his friends. He himself, however, was aware of the danger which still encompassed him and so he gave them a signal with his hand to keep silent and then recounted to them the incomprehensible event in which he had personally participated.

It is of special significance when Peter declares that *the Lord himself had led him out of prison.* He knew that it was Christ

Jesus, the Exalted Lord himself, who had snatched him from the impending danger of death. For Jesus was present to the apostle in the person of the " angel of the Lord " who seemingly performed the task. Constantly the Acts of the Apostles relates such belief in the presence of the Lord and shows how it shaped the church's every act and dictated her conduct.

The report which Peter gave must have imprinted itself indelibly on the group that had gathered together to pray; and we may conjecture that the description which Luke offers preserved intact the liveliness of the story with which Peter himself must have regaled them.

Tell this to James and to the brothers. This statement has given rise to a variety of explanations. Who is this James? Without doubt he is one of those who played an important role in the community of Jerusalem. He is the same one whom we will later on encounter at the Council of the Apostles as a representative of a compromising policy in the problem of missionary activity to the gentiles. When Paul returned from his third missionary journey (21 : 18), he visited James and was advised by him to offer a sacrifice of purification in the temple. He thought that by this act Paul could pacify the hostile Jews. According to all, he is the same James whom Paul mentions more than a few times in his letter to the Galatians. He is a " brother " of the Lord (Gal. 1 : 19) and is numbered among the " pillars of the church " (Gal. 2 : 9), and he is also a disciple of the party which advocated strict observance of the law in the Judeo-Christian church (Gal. 2 : 12). We do not exclude—and by so doing do not seek to minimize the difficulty of the problem—the possibility that this James, whom Peter calls by name, is to be regarded as an apostle and as such occupied an important post in guiding the community of Jerusalem.

When Peter mentions the " brothers " along with James, he may well have meant the other apostles and together with them the elders (the presbyters), if there were any at the moment in Jerusalem. But what is the " announcement " which *James and the brethren* should receive? Primarily, of course, it is information about what Peter had experienced during the course of his rescue. Along with that there was, we are inclined to think, a *warning* about the danger which also threatened them. As long as Peter occupied the throne, the church, and especially the leaders of the church, were the prey of Herod Agrippa, even though they observed the Jewish law as this had been taught to them by James. James, the brother of John, had been beheaded; Peter had narrowly escaped the same fate. What was there to hinder Agrippa from seeking out the remaining members of the infant community in an attempt to gain the goodwill of the Jews?

Then he departed to another place. Peter fled from Jerusalem while it was still night. His personal security made such haste on his part imperative. He simply acted in accordance with an admonition which Jesus himself had proposed: " When they persecute you in one city, flee to another " (Mt. 10:23). To what city did he flee? Why does Luke fail to give us its precise name for this is contrary to his usual literary style, since in many of his narratives he names both the time and the place of the salvation events?

Punishment of the Persecutor (12:15-23)

[18]*When day dawned, a by no means minor dispute arose among the soldiers over what had happened to Peter.* [19]*And when*

Herod despatched a search party after him, without finding him, he tried the sentries and then ordered them to be put to death. And he took himself off to Caesarea to remain there. [20]He was filled with anger at the inhabitants of Tyre and Sidon; but they appeared before him in a body and after having persuaded Blastus, the chamberlain, they sued for peace; for their lands depended for their provender on that of the king. [21]On an appointed day, Herod, robed in kingly apparel, took his place on the dais and addressed the people. [22]The people shouted, " This is the voice of a god, not a man." [23]But the angel of the Lord immediately struck him on that very spot, because he did not give glory to God. Consumed by worms, he gave up his spirit.

It may surprise us that Luke places the story of the death of Herod at the end of his narrative, dealing as it does with the development of the church. His purpose is, however, easily detectable. *Herod and the church* are shown to be in opposition to one another throughout the whole conclusion of chapter 12. Danger and decay menace the church. The first apostle falls a victim to the power of Herod, to the applause of many among the Jews. The church would have been dealt a terrible blow had Peter succumbed, that is to say, if the will of Herod had been fulfilled. We do not know, of course, what further plans had been devised by this monarch. But if his treachery were to be effective, it would have been necessary to destroy the entire church.

With the help of God, Peter slipped away from out the death-dealing hands of Herod. Now the persecutor punished the soldiers, and withdrew to the city where he usually resided. Did he devote any thought to the unusual manner by which the prisoner apostle escaped? Did he as an afterthought abandon his plans for further persecutions? We do not know. It is important, however, for Luke to show us how this man died, for to Luke it is a fitting symbol, because it demonstrates so strikingly the irresistibility, the invincibility of the church and the power of the punishing hand of God which stretches out heavily to fall upon all who would inflict damage upon his body. The condemnation of Herod is closely connected with his overweaning display of external prestige and pomp.

The reconciliation with Tyre and Sidon affords an opportunity for a solemn festival. The king appears in all his regal pomp by which his political power is ostentatiously displayed. He awaits the applause of his audience. They sense the vanity of their ruler. They show him divine honors. " The voice of God, and not of a man," they cry out in shameless flattery, as he stands on the platform before them. Let us pause for a moment to consider the contrast here to that greeting which Peter received from Cornelius, the Roman centurion. Cornelius wished to acknowledge the divine honors that had been bestowed upon the apostle. And Peter brushes it aside: " Get up. I also am only a man " (10:26).

Herod, the caricatured god of the people, experiences in his own person the punishment meted out by one to whom he refused to pay what he and he alone deserves and merits. The answer of the true Lord of creation is given to him on the spot. He suffers a dreadful death. We do not know the nature of the sickness which in the language of the people was popularly designated as " to be eaten by worms," but it reminds us of the description of that malady from which the Syrian king, Antiochus Epiphanes IV, suffered for his crimes against the Jewish people (Mac. 9:5ff.).

The Church Presses Forward (12:24-25)

²⁴*But the word of God unfolded its power and propagated itself far and wide.* ²⁵*Barnabas, however, and Saul, after fulfilling their mission, returned from Jerusalem, bringing with them John whose other name was Mark.*

A brief note concludes the description of the establishment and the development of the church at Antioch. It is a résumé such as Luke is accustomed to insert between narratives. The church grows apace; the " word of God " or, as we could actually translate it according to another textual version, " the word of the Lord," unfolds its power. An indestructible life principle is stored within it. It is the life power of the Risen and Exalted Lord, the power of the Holy Spirit, whom the Risen One had promised to his church when he commissioned the apostles to be witnesses to him from the confines of Jerusalem to the ends of the earth (1:8). We saw the witness of the apostle from town to town; we saw the power which makes the message and the charism of miracles so effective. We saw how the people, listening attentively and believing whole-heartedly, submitted to the word. We saw also how resistance and persecution were placed in the path of witnesses to no avail. We saw how danger and destruction menaced the church even from within. But the Spirit of the church filled, enlightened, and strengthened her all during this troublesome time. And this power will be with her as she henceforth prepares and makes herself ready for the missionary effort that she is about to inaugurate. In the last sentence of the interjected explanatory note, we read the names of Barnabas and Saul together with that of the cousin of Barnabas, John-Mark.

The enumeration of these names serves as a kind of position paper. Barnabas and Saul, the two friends, take the road from Jerusalem back to Damascus in order to be able the more quickly to leave for the " work for which the Holy Spirit had called them " (13 : 2).

The message of salvation has now started on its road and will continue to move forward uninterruptedly. To demonstrate the invincibility of the word has been the purpose of the Lucan narrative thus far; to emphasize it is the reason behind all that follows.